Travels in
the
Unknown East

Travels in
the
Unknown East

by
JOHN GRANT

THE OCTAGON PRESS
LONDON

ISBN 0 863040 71 3

First published 1992

Photoset, printed and bound by
Redwood Press, Melksham, Wiltshire

Contents

Preface

Over five decades ago, I made the first journeys recorded in this book. Now that this half-century is over, I am freed from the promises made then to avoid certain names and topics.

When the time came to write this book, it was surprising to find how many things had hardly changed at all.

The thinking of people in the Near and Middle East has hardly shifted. And this in spite of sweeping, often cataclysmic, change in its regimes, life-styles and appearances.

All the odder when one recalls that many of the friends from my early journeys are now into their old age. Then they were in their twenties.

And – unlike their supposedly better-informed Western contemporaries – so many had accurately predicted how their lives, their countries and their own destinies would move.

I am convinced that many Eastern people have a reliable guiding sense of human directions. This beats all the science, the theories and the systems of the West. But what further can one say than that?

Perhaps it is because we of the Occident prize orderly theories and attempt, vainly, to live by trying things out rather than by knowledge: while, of course, imagining that we are behaving otherwise.

Perhaps all that I am saying has, indeed, already been articulated, in more succinct form as: *Ex oriente lux.*

John Grant
Omdurman, October 1991

Children of
The Golden Horn

CONSTANTINOPLE! There is magic in the name.

There was a thin, silken, gossamer haze, lazily floating over the deep blue of the Sea of Marmara.

In the distance, luxuriantly shimmering in the eastern sunlight, were low-lying hills. Here and there came a glint of gold as the sun's rays caught and reflected the glory of an elegantly-domed mosque.

Tall and white, and as sentinels looking out upon these waters of destiny and centuries of tragedy, were slender minarets, symbolic of the Crescent and its vast fields of slumbering power.

Not so long ago this was Constantinople, the capital of the mighty Ottoman Empire and home of the Sultans, the emperors of the Turkish dominions, and the Caliphs: successors to the Prophet.

The centre, the hub, of the great Moslem world. Its religious edicts were obeyed from North Africa to Java. It was known as the City of Enchantment and as the Diamond of the Orient.

Now it is merely Istanbul, secondary in importance to

the newly-created capital of Ankara, which was until recently, little more than an Anatolian village.

The famous bejewelled palaces of the Sultans are public museums now. The last of the Sultans has gone. With a few treasures screwed up in a newspaper, he fled into the blackness of the night and sought refuge upon a British man-of-war.

And then he was subsisting in penury in an insignificant villa in Switzerland. Later on his daughter married the son of the richest man in the world – His Exalted Highness, the Nizam of Hyderabad – and the son-in-law made easier the lot of the ex-monarch: the former Shadow of Allah Upon Earth, Master of the Sublime Gateway . . .

As I walked the length of the Galata Bridge, which connects the more modern city with the old, I looked instinctively for those characteristic touches I remembered so well.

As the scene unfolded however, I seemed to be thinking more of America! Turkey – modern Turkey – had changed.

Not so long ago, the berries of Fez dyed red (and gave their city's name to) the brimless headgear of every Turk. And every Turk, too, would wear flowing Eastern raiment. The curly-toed Turkish slipper fell softly on the cobblestones of the winding bazaar streets.

There was a bewitching cadence in the light, silvery footsteps of those who gazed, sometimes with provokingly roguish eyes, from behind the impenetrable sanctuary of the half-veil.

Then, and it was still in living memory, on the Holy Friday of each week, the Sultan rode in state to the Mosque. There was colour. There was pageantry.

Scarlet-clad lancers, undefeated in war, mounted upon some of the finest horses in Europe, swept majestically along before the Royal carriage. The people bent their heads in salutation, not so much to the Sultan, but to that dual personality, the Emperor who was Caliph of all Islam.

Now, all this was swept aside. Instead, there was the law of Ataturk: Father of the Turks. He had decreed the fez to be an emblem of servitude and national weakness.

Turkey was no longer to be a nation which drew its strength primarily from religion. The fez gave way to the bowler hat and the Homburg. The flowing garments went, to make room for the reach-me-down. With her veil gone, the Turkish damsel now bargained at the store.

She has grown in stature also – thanks to high-heeled shoes, excessively Parisian in conception, which now adorned or maltreated her feet depending on the point of view.

Why drag the United States into all this? Because I do not think that there would have been these dramatic changes but for President Wilson.

In 1918, after the First World War, when the Ottoman Empire lay sprawling in the dust like some great, winded colossus, the great majority of Turks looked to America to assume a Mandate, some sort of protectorate, over the truncated State.

A deputation was sent to Washington to this end, not because Turkey was enamoured of America; but because many felt that President Wilson of the freedom-loving USA was more friendly than was Mr. Lloyd George, heir to imperialist thinking.

Nothing came of it, although the subject was seriously

considered. The USA, of course, can consider herself well out of what would have been a horrible mess. Had she accepted the mandate, she would have had to support the Sultan and the Government in Constantinople against the rising forces of revolution under Mustafa Kemal, the Ghazi [Islamic Hero] who was soon to be the leader of his nation.

What the final outcome would have been is a matter for conjecture. Certain it is, however, that in many fundamental ways present-day Turkey would be very different.

The two opposing forces – the Sultanate, the Sublime Porte, and revolutionary Ankara – were finely balanced. The intrusion of another element would have swayed the forces of war and changed the destinies of many millions.

And so, the Western cap became the symbol of modern Turkey. As a symbol it causes one to think again of what might have been if America had accepted that mandate. The baseball cap would surely not have looked more incongruous.

The peaks of Western caps are a constant source of worry and annoyance to the Turks. They fidget with them as does an irritable man with a nagging tooth.

It is as if the average Turk wants to tear away the peak could he but summon up the requisite moral courage. More often than not he seeks to hide it from view. He droops it over one ear. When the peak incommodes the ear, it is pushed round to the back of the neck.

And the women? They have gone far. They have come out from the shelter of the veil and have adopted the coat and skirt. They still don't much like hats, though. Millinery shops quickly went bankrupt in modern Istanbul, when they opened up in dozens in the first flush of republican and counter-Islamic fervour. The women tie their hair in a multicoloured scarf, descendant of the veil, and leave it at that.

Soon the younger generation of Turkish women was beginning to insist upon a place in industry. They were, by the early 1930s, to be found behind receptionists' counters in the hotels, and beginning to pound typewriters: they began to walk in the streets unattended and found to their surprise that they were left unmolested . . .

They even discovered that they had elbows: and the uses to which these could be put when places on public vehicles were scarce. I have yet to tell the difference in effect between an elbow in the ribs on the sunlit streets of ancient Istanbul and one received when on the gloomy platforms of the Piccadilly Underground or the New York Subway.

Inasmuch as the greatest social change in Turkey has been effected by liberating the women there, I took the opportunity to investigate that facet of latter-day Turkey a decade or so after these changes had been instituted.

I wanted to meet both the old and the new women of Istanbul; and so I contrived to meet both at one and the same time. Thanks to an introduction to 'one of the Old School', I met both her and her silk-hosed granddaughter – one of the emancipated women: it was literally a case of a meeting of extremes.

Zobeda met me timidly, for I was one of those beings still to be kept at a respectable distance – a man. Many years of incarceration behind the walls of her lord's seraglio had rendered her incapable of meeting the world. She found it well-nigh impossible to face the realities of a landscape changed so drastically by the Young Turks.

I had no great difficulty in bringing about this meeting with one reputed to be a recluse. My grandfather had known her father in the old, imperial days. They were both Sufis, from that worldwide community whose members – according to one's prejudice – were strange cultists, apostates or the true, enlightened mystics: perceptive of the secrets transcending all faiths.

Zobeda was undoubtedly one of the few surviving women of her type. There were plenty of emancipated, modernist women here, but I wanted contrast, the more easily to determine exactly how far the women of Turkey who had assimilated the new thought were from the old ways.

Although the revolutionary changes brought about by the republican regime in Turkey are truly staggering, it must be said that no hand has been stretched towards depriving anybody of property which was rightfully theirs, or even of taking away well-merited prestige. So Zobeda retained her fairly large estate to the full under the new order, and was allowed to live her life in her own way.

As I stepped into the courtyard of her palatial house, surrounded as it was by wonderful old-world gardens, I thought that within those walls the twentieth century might not have dawned at all.

The air was heavy with scented citron blossom; sycamore trees stood like sentinels around the outer wall as if guarding the harem, and yellowish-brown cinnamon trees lined the marble pathway to the fountain in the centre of the garden. Here we sat in the chequered shade of an arboreal vine.

The present-day outdoor garb of all Turkish women is the same – shall I say by law? – as that of any European woman in London or Paris. But when Zobeda received me at her home near Istanbul she wore the clothes that she used to wear in Imperial times.

They were both colourful and becoming so that I took particular notice.

On her head she wore a small red velvet cap, encircled by a beautifully embroidered handkerchief of green silk, over which strings of pearls and tiny gold coins were attached like festoons. On the top of this skullcap was a diamond clasp in the shape of a crescent, from which there hung a long tassel of gold thread strung with pearls and rubies.

Over her long skirt was a close-fitting vest, highly ornamented and laced in front with thick gold braid. Her long loose trousers narrowed to the ankles, and she wore an elegant, long-fringed and costly shawl.

Her eyes, though old, were radiant as big black diamonds, and her finger-nails were reddened with henna.

Zobeda spoke to me in Persian, the language of culture of the Ottoman court, and then in Arabic; and continued a more heated argument in French. She told me that during her youth no woman of education in Turkey was qualified to 'grace her husband's home' unless she were a good cook, a good horse-rider and a conversationalist; but, above all, she had to know several languages.

A servant girl brought real Turkish coffee, very strong and with lots of sugar; another bore a tray full of fresh and dried fruits; and a third, slices of iced melon. From each she tasted a little, and then passed them on to me.

'Allah is bountiful,' she said: the signal for me to eat.

'You see,' she continued, 'it was the custom in some families for the hostess to taste the food before the guests, so that visitors could be quite sure that the food contained nothing objectionable. There was so much talk of poisoning, ground glass and the like, in our earlier years. Today, this tasting is merely a convention.'

I touched my forehead in salutation, then passed my hand to my eyes and to my heart, connoting in Turkish

7

fashion that the head, the eyes and heart were all at the service of my hostess.

Emboldened by her many courtesies, and bent upon reaching the truth, I asked whether it *was* not really a life in a gilded cage that she had lived for thirty years before the freeing of Turkish women.

Her eyes narrowed a little as if remembering. This old lady's eyes were now full of an ancient's memories; they seemed stronger for things a long way off. Then she spoke and her gaze was piercing.

'I do agree that it was a cage – but, in my case at least, a very large cage.' Her recollection went back to the dawn of the century.

'You may notice that the extent of my place here is more than forty acres. A house of sixty rooms, a garden with a lake, a horse-riding track, room for everything.

'In the morning I would ride with my three sisters, after lunch I could walk miles in my garden, and I could go anywhere on the shores of the Bosphorus and even up to the Black Sea, fully escorted by my servants and retainers.

'I could receive visits from lady friends, and visit them in their homes; I played and danced for my lord, the Pasha, in the harem. Remember, Western people who criticize without knowledge, do not even know the simplest things about it: for instance, that "Harem" means "Holy Place". And I was loved by the Pasha. One man's love was enough for me. They say it is not the same in the West: but at least those of us who do not know Western Europe do not attack it.

'You see that?' she motioned, directing my attention to the farthest end of a spacious arcade surrounded by a dome-shaped structure, its cornice ornamented with Turkish inscriptions.

'There I used to dine with my lord after he came home

from his duties with the Sultan; and there, under the lingering moon, I danced for him – for him alone. I played the flute and he, my loving husband, poured gold coins into my lap – and I was happy, very happy.'

Tears welled in her eyes as she dreamed of her romance, her life of peace and protection, as she termed it.

The old lady thought that the liberty that she had enjoyed gave her ample scope. She was trained to remain in the sphere of womanhood, to be a good mother and a good wife – the house her domain; protected from the rough and tumble of the world, to be loved and cared for.

In her view, there could be no discussion of the equality of the sexes. The spheres of the two had been made separate by Nature. In the time of her youth, the women of Turkey did not have to shoulder responsibilities of a grosser type; for she considered engaging in business, or service of any sort, to be definitely beneath the dignity of womanhood.

Her sole object was to be 'one of the mothers of the nation', to keep her lord and family in good health, to look after the haven which a man wants after the day's hard work, to bring up her children in the best traditions of her folk, 'for the woman was the mother of man'.

As long as the mother could be the custodian of a man's interests and activities, just so long, she emphasized, would the reality and traditions of her people remain.

She had eighteen servants and six slave girls. The tempo of life was not rapid, but her days were happy.

'But the whole scene,' she said, as her granddaughter joined us, 'sometimes appears now like an absurd dream. Things have changed here in tune with the shifting times; we have had to come into line with the rest of the world.'

Her granddaughter, dressed in a designer's creation, with short hair and a cigarette between her lips, then spoke her mind. She, like everybody in Turkey, was a hero-worshipper – her heart was deservedly at the feet of the President of their Republic, Kemal Ataturk.

'Think what he has done for us – this one man made Turkey live at a time when Turkey was all but dead.'

Here she reminded me that, after the First World War, when their nation had been practically wiped out as a power, there was famine and disease, murder and brigandage; 'the whole nation was made to crawl as slaves'.

The fabric of a new nation had to be built up. Kemal started to build, fought wars, reclaimed the lost heritage – won for Turkey the right to live again as a self-respecting nation; while the colonial Powers 'salivated outside a locked door'.

The world had gone ahead; women of the New Turkey had to come and to help their menfolk to rebuild, to take their share in all the walks of life. The unveiling of women was but a superficial sign of progress.

With the ardent passion of youth, Zobeda's granddaughter told me that at last, after centuries in the seraglio, Turkish women had an opportunity to prove that they should not be 'buried behind harem walls. Their place is in the front rank of general national activity,' she said.

When I returned to Turkey, decades later, I met this lady again. Now a grey-haired, dynamic grandmother herself, she was campaigning for her country's entry into the European Common Market, with all the vigour that she had shown that day, almost at the dawn of Kemal's republic.

In banks all over Turkey, innumerable girls were working, even in the early days of the new regime. There were more than two thousand women doctors and an equal number of women in the professions of law and education.

There were women police, women authors, journalists and publishers. Eight thousand six hundred new schools and colleges for girls had been entirely staffed with qualified Turkish teachers. Even a tank and machine-gun corps existed – run and maintained by women. In civil flying, women pilots had covered more than half of Asiatic Turkey by the mid nineteen-twenties.

In the arts, women of the new Turkey have found few equals, and practically all the best embroidery done in the Near East today is commissioned from the Istanbul Art College.

Marriage is no longer regarded as the only career, but home life is still held in high esteem.

The freedom of the women of Turkey was regarded by this young girl as the right type of freedom; and to the chagrin of many a Turkish diehard who prophesied the worst, the women have made good.

The slogan has it that the future of Turkey rests with her women. From what I saw of it in Istanbul, Constantinople that was, I have no hesitation in saying that that future is bright.

Bewildering as is the effort of blending the old with the new, I observed that many of the essentials of Turkish tradition remain the same. I went to view the ancient citadel standing upon the even more ancient site of the Acropolis.

Entering through the principal gate, I came immediately into an exquisite garden stretching right down to the sea-front. This is now a public park to which mothers wheel their children in up-to-date perambulators. Soldiers gravitate there, to show off their uniforms.

Upon a hill are the kiosks of the palace. Rows of cypress

trees indicate the way to the inner palace. The trees, silent reminders of an age-old pageantry, lead directly to the Gate of Felicity where, standing in the portico, the courtiers were wont to kiss the hand of their Sultan.

On the left is the old Diwan: the Audience-Chamber resembling the famous Hall of Private Audience, in Delhi. Behind all this is the Imperial Harem.

Even now, after the lapse of years, one approaches with a certain amount of trepidation. The walls seem to radiate atmosphere; one can feel the sense of bliss and tragedy which the stones reflect. The dramas enacted there were too real, too intense, too gripping and too vibrant for the easy dissipation of their reactions.

There are the watch-holes at the entrance where the grim-faced eunuchs kept ceaseless vigil. From there a dark passage leads to the living-rooms of this dispersed legion. In this passage more than one unwanted wife met a sudden death with a silken cord around her neck. That, at any rate, is the tradition. In reality, nobody knows how much of this sombre story was concocted by enemies of the Ottomans. As a conquering empire, they certainly had plenty of opponents.

The harem proper is a fantastic collection of both large and small rooms. Each is furnished with costly divans and tiny tables. The doors are of mother-of-pearl and ivory and are exquisitely worked. Marble baths and basins are everywhere, but the fountains which once poured their silvery cascades are now silent.

Screens of wonderfully pierced, wafer-thin marble cover the windows.

This was the home of many hundreds of beautiful women. The majority, it is said, fought among themselves for supremacy and the attentions of their royal master.

Some who found their way there through dark and mysterious channels were said to have eaten ground glass and poisonous herbs rather than await the summons to the royal chamber.

Away from the harem, there are the rooms of the Sultan, packed with the worldly goods of a departed monarchy. There are golden cups, costly tapestries, daggers, bejewelled belts and royal garments. There is the glistening throne of Shah Ismail of Persia, captured by Sultan Selim in 1514. It is of gold, and is inlaid with rubies and emeralds. As a seat for the mighty it must have been amazingly uncomfortable.

All around are the mute witnesses of a period of four hundred years in the history of Turkey. The whole is a museum of memories.

Not so far away is the fortified castle of the Seven Towers. This too, echoes the misery and the tragedies of the past. One enters through a triumphal arch, but there is little of triumph attaching to this gruesome pile.

The place is one mass of ghastly, black dungeons, the walls worn smooth by the almost continuous procession of the condemned which found its way there. Men of high estate met their deaths in these pestilential holes. Here even Sultans have had their heads swept from their bodies with one stroke of a sword.

As it is related, admittedly by detractors, there was one monarch whose death was particularly horrible. His mother crept up on him in the night and strangled him with her own hands.

Here there is a rectangular room filled with wooden cages. In these prisoners were kept, huddled like battery-hens, until they were taken out to be slaughtered in full view of the other prisoners.

Nearby is the Pit of Blood. Here men were made to

crane their necks over the side of the pit. A sword gleamed, and the head fell into the red pool below.

By the pit there are stakes. Around the stakes, at about the height of a man's heart, there are bullet holes in the walls.

All this is new history growing out of the old, as history always does. But what is essentially ancient will live for ever in Turkey as elsewhere. And one of the most hoary institutions is the bazaar.

There are electrically lit markets, there are old and indescribably decrepit bazaars, there are clusters of booths hurriedly put up; there are vendors who carry their wares on trays or stand beside trolleys of perfume bottles, nuts and rosaries . . .

But in spirit and colourfulness old and new are all astonishingly similar.

In that vaulted bazaar, the Covered Market, for instance, one can buy the costliest jewel here: and there, in the next shop – it might be a cobbler's – there humanity surges like the very waves of the Golden Horn.

Every known language it seems, is being spoken. A bright cummerbund decorates a frock-coat. A turbaned man of Kurdistan is trying to make a Turkish shopkeeper understand that the price he asks is at least five times what the Kurd is prepared to pay.

'Go to a shrine then,' shouts the shopkeeper back at his customer, 'and pray that gold may grow on the bushes to let you buy what you want!'

After much coffee-drinking at the booth, the offer is clinched, both smile, and the Kurd ties the ring in the tail of his turban, only to find that deft fingers are soon trying to open the knot as he makes his way through the throng.

A number of idle spectators listen, trying to understand what an American tourist might want with an old, rusty sword, for which he is bargaining hotly with a Greek vendor. Neither knows the other's language very well, and the wit of the American's guide cannot adequately translate the jibes of the shopkeeper, either.

A few paces on, men and women are sipping coffee, that real coffee which only the Turk can make, with a great deal of sugar and no milk; others are eating sliced melons, and yet another is wrapping syrupy honey and pastry sweetmeats in his handkerchief.

There is raucous noise, there is laughter, and even an occasional exchange of hot words, which soon dies down as the bargain is struck; till the policeman comes round to tell you that within a quarter of an hour the bazaar will be shut and you had better leave: lighting-up time outside was two hours ago.

All the same, if the more strictly controlled bazaars have to close at a respectable hour, you can still enjoy the bustle in others a little more remote from the centre of town.

A bazaar is a place about as symbolic of an Oriental city as Piccadilly might be of London, or Times Square of New York. It is the club of the people; it is the one place in the town where you can gossip and not be taken seriously.

The very name 'bazaar' conjures up a scene of mysterious traffickings and an environment of colour and adventure.

How many romances, Western and Oriental, have had their beginning in bazaars, and how many unwritten adventures have had their inception in those romantic caves of commerce?

A market in Europe is merely a market. But a bazaar may be the gateway to Paradise or to the opposite, for any man at any moment.

The long, shaded vistas of these mercantile galleries, the babel of voices which arises in them, the vocabulary of protest, of cajolery, of insistence, in which these voices are couched; the drench and fall of heat, of fragrance, of less worthy odours; the emanations of rapacity, scorn, cunning and hatred they give forth – and in their strange withdrawnness, the profoundly mystical sense which they evoke of something as old as time: these things serve to place 'bazaars' among the more wonderful of human institutions, the very stuff of imagination.

To enter a bazaar anywhere between say, Istanbul and Rangoon, is to enter a place imbued with the self-same passions and experiences. And surely, this bazaar of which I am writing is merely a replica of all the thousands of bazaars or *souks* in Arabia, in Egypt, in India, in Afghanistan or anywhere.

The trading methods, the craftsmanship of the East, are virtually one; a jeweller, a carpenter in Egypt may be a jeweller and carpenter in Turkestan or in India. The local fashions may differ, but the methods of working and selling are the same.

The little booth with its jumbled display of goods or articles, the generally bearded human who presides over its destinies, these are ever the same. Time has touched them no more than the everlasting rocks of Damascus in Syria or the forests which hang above Tiblisi in Caucasia.

A thousand years' passing cannot bring any change to the face of an Oriental bazaar: if change comes, then Eastern emotion will cease to be, and Asia's soul will assuredly be dead!

Though the Covered Market may have closed, life is still throbbing in Pera – formerly considered the main European quarter – though the atmosphere is scarcely Turkish. In the cabarets and dance-halls there, I would not have imagined that I was in Istanbul. It would vie with the nightlife of Paris or Amsterdam, any day.

But modernization notwithstanding, an average Turk even now will spit noisily when you speak to him about what goes on in Pera.

'That is not Turkish, that Pera,' he would say scornfully, 'I would deal with my daughter if I found her there after dark', and leave you to make your own deductions from his remarks.

The post-revolutionary Turk now had no harem to go to, no place for that customary little concert of an evening. He soon sought the nightlife and the society of the thousands of dubious ladies of foreign origin who swarmed into the former Turkish capital – Russian refugees, needy Central and Eastern Europeans, Circassians, and even freed slaves who would formerly have been sold in the market-place – indeed, such a motley picture of femininity as surely no city in the world can ever have witnessed.

These conditions naturally lent themselves to the machinations of the many international criminals who had always haunted the city when it was an imperial capital, and who now sought to profit from the new state of affairs.

With vultures' eyes they saw a paradise of beautiful, unprotected women, many of high rank and great attractions, and all entirely at their mercy. Who would miss a ruined Russian countess or the discarded wife of a former Pasha in the turmoil of the nineteen-twenties and -thirties?

So there began a hideous and soul-destroying trade: the detestable wholesale traffic in kidnapped women, sold as slaves to the stews of the Levant. Or, in some cases, even traded to buyers in Istanbul itself.

And what of today? With the breakup of the Communist State in the USSR, just to the North, and the tumbling of the socialist regimes of Eastern Europe, on Turkey's doorstep, fresh floods of dubious and penniless people have entered the city. Is the pattern of vice of sixty and seventy years before in danger of being repeated?

Yes, it is a changed Istanbul. On my last visit there I could scarcely recognize what was once for practical purposes a city of men. It is that no longer.

Constantinople, once the sacred city of the Turk, is now the Paris of the East, without perhaps the brio and dash of Paris. For the Easterner is too grave to throw himself into the puerile gaiety and the superficial airs of the French capital. He cannot dance too well. He tends to shrink from the disco.

He has no objection, however, to the *houris* of the Arabian nights, or to talking to them in the language of exaggerated poetry, telling them that their eyes are like the reflection of the stars in the water of the Golden Horn, or their cheeks like the roses of Ispahan. So his dance-halls are rather a failure, beautiful though their foreign co-ryphées may be.

In the early days of the Republic, visiting Istanbul, one kept one's nose clean and tended to avoid the seamier side of life.

I had heard, of course, of the widespread practice of kidnapping Turkish and other women of rank who had been newly-emancipated from the veil and the seraglio. Yet I had given the matter only passing thought until it thrust itself upon me one day with all the crude shock of reality.

It was a Friday, and I had indulged in a Turkish bath at a well-known establishment in the rather sordid and absurdly named Grand Rue.

It had been a very good bath. And, after cooling off, I was enjoying a rest in the garden behind the establishment. A fountain was tinkling musically, and it was cool and shady in the little arbour where I sat.

Suddenly I heard a voice in French not many yards away – a man's voice. I caught every syllable distinctly, though the words were scarcely above a whisper.

I realised with a shock, when I absorbed the words, that this was the voice of a cultivated man or an aristocrat.

'They come here every Friday by car at three o'clock precisely. I shall dispose of their transport somehow. We will have a taxi at the door. Today week, and you shall drive, you hear? I shall tell them that their car has had an accident. They will naturally enter the conveyance, and you will drive at top speed to where the fast launch lies. You understand?'

'Yes, but will it be worth the risk?'

'I should say so. Nobody suspects us. And have you seen them!? We shall take them straight to Izmir.'

'But the husband is a wealthy man. Why not hold both the women to ransom?'

'Altogether too dangerous. I want to get back to Athens with a whole skin, and you to Trieste, I suppose, with a full purse. Now listen . . .'

That was all I heard. The two at this point left their seats, and as I rose I caught only a rear view of them, vanishing into a crowd. But it was sufficient. I would remember them again. I would be present at the little interview they had planned.

Next Friday, therefore, I made a point of being on guard at the door of the baths at three o'clock. I had not long to wait. Soon a handsome car, a large Citroën, drew up. Two tall, exquisitely-dressed young ladies alighted and entered the establishment.

When they were safely inside, I turned to the chauffeur who had driven them.

'Please be on your guard,' I said. 'There is a plot to capture your mistress and her friend. Do not leave this place on any pretext.'

The Frenchman became very excited, and asked a dozen half-formed questions. I hushed him and told him all I knew, and his mouth hardened as he calmed down.

'So that's it?' he murmured. 'Well, we shall see.'

Some five minutes later one of the conspirators emerged from the baths and hailed the chauffeur in French. I winked and nodded to the manservant, putting him on the *qui vive*.

'I am the manager,' said the wily chief woman-snatcher in oily accents. 'Your mistress has asked me to tell you not to wait. She has plans for this afternoon. You may drive home.'

The chauffeur regarded him steadily for a moment, then raising his foot in the manner of the French *savateur*, dealt the scoundrel such a hearty kick in the stomach that he doubled up and fell groaning in agony to the pavement, where he received still further savage treatment from the enraged Parisian.

At last, screaming and blaspheming, the white slaver picked himself up and hobbled off, pursued for many yards by the infuriated driver.

Soon the ladies reappeared, and I heaved a sigh of relief when I saw them enter their car safely. But for how long were they safe, I asked myself, in such a city?

So Istanbul jazzes, or pretends to jazz; the nightlife continues beneath the coloured lamps and the young Turks believe they have imported a Western atmosphere.

The tourists pour into Istanbul, yet the Turks, on the whole, retain a great deal of their former dignity. Generally what there is of the undesirable is what has come flooding in with modernisation, Europeans and tourists; rather than, as generally supposed, being due to the viciousness of the East.

What a sad commentary on Western civilization!

2

The Heart of Turkey

When one leaves Istanbul and makes for Anatolia, it seems like going into a different world.

Eskishehr – a dusty, poverty-striken village, yet a name, nevertheless. The Greeks never mention it without spitting. The Turk intones it with a kind of reverence. The Greeks, when they occupied Asia Minor after the First War, advanced beyond Eskishehr. In their retreat they demolished one half of the town and set fire to the rest.

It was here that General Mustafa Kemal Pasha achieved his greatest victory and set the seal upon his ascendancy. Here one can still recapture some of the spirit of that struggle. When I first saw it, less than ten years after the First War, there were roofless and shapeless structures still begrimed with smoke, but reconstruction was going on.

In Eskishehr they still regarded the stranger with some suspicion. One had to carry a passport everywhere and even then was liable to be hauled off, with the greatest politeness it is true, to the police station for interrogation.

On one of my many enforced marches to the police station, the way led past a café. The policeman suggested coffee and, what is more, had the grace to pay for it also! Is it cupboard love, or am I just impressed by the civilised behaviour of the ordinary Turk?

At the police station, after a nervous official had asked me my business and had fingered a passport he was obviously incapable of reading, I was invited to a room at the rear of the station. Here I was regaled with melon, more coffee, and Oriental sweets and delicious pistachio halwa.

The officer who apprehended me acted as waiter!

In the hills beyond Eskishehr is Ankara – the sixty-year-old home of the new Turkey. On arriving at the railway station, the first thing which you see is the wall built by the conqueror, Timur the Lame – Tamerlane.

As to the town itself: on a steep rocky hill about five hundred feet in height, there are rows upon rows of houses, mostly of brick, stuck upon its sides as if growing out of a mound. The ancient wall surrounds the old section of the city; and the dry plains which surround that give it a desolate air.

Soon however, your eyes alight upon the broad avenues, and tall buildings 'kissing the feet' of the rocky eminences of Ankara. These stately buildings – government offices, hotels, the parliament house, various embassies: they leave you in no doubt that Turkey is going ahead.

'Your chief problem here is water?' I asked an official of the new regime. An old soldier of Turkey who had been fighting for his country since he was fifteen years old, he seemed to take my innocent remark somewhat unkindly.

'We have had few years of real peace here,' he replied brusquely. 'Give us time. Give us time.'

However when I praised the results of even those few

years of effort in making the desertlike Ankara blossom, he warmed.

He was proud of the reconstruction going on and pointed out the installation of a very powerful radio station, public parks, avenues and boulevards; and 'Look at this hotel', in the lounge of which we were talking.

It might have been in the heart of a fashionable European capital; its charges were certainly half what you pay in a London hotel of the same status. And on top of that, I as a teetotaller, did not have any wines or spirits, so the room rate was reduced by a third for me.

I admired the belly-dancer of the hotel's widely trumpeted Folkloric Evening. The old man (a former Pasha – all titles had been abolished) fixed me with a stern gaze. 'Do you think that that woman is Turkish?' he asked. I could not answer.

'Hear and note particularly,' he leant towards me, 'that this is a Viennese dancer. Not a Turkish woman. We have not debased ourselves to quite that extent yet.' He looked as if he were about to spit.

'And the abolishing of the veil?' I parried.

'Ah, that had to come one day. It was the Law of the Ghazi. My Ghazi, Ataturk!'

A sudden memory, as he put it, rang in his brain like a chime from a distant tower. After my promising not to reveal his name, he agreed to tell me what chord had struck in his heart when he thought of his hero – the Ataturk – the mighty Ghazi – whom all Turks love. As a historical document with so much of human courage and dignity, this is his story.

'Well, it was many years ago,' he began, as if in a reverie, 'I would not worry about the exact date, but I remember having rushed to Baron's Hotel in Aleppo, and finding Mustafa Kemal Pasha, later our President of the

Turkish Republic, pacing up and down the dining-room in a thoughtful mood.

'The military situation seemed hopeless. I begged him to flee, for English troops had already entered the outskirts of the city.

'He motioned me to keep quiet, and after being told that all his men had withdrawn in safety, even his bodyguard, he ordered me to pull down the blinds of the room overlooking the road. Then he whispered a command: "Leave me alone, and hide yourself as you can: as for me," he smiled, "my death is still very far off."

'Presently we saw the figures of three Arabs flit past the deserted hotel like ghosts, chased by some yelling troopers of the British Indian cavalry.

'"Go, and hide yourself, you fool," again huskily commanded Kemal.

'"I go where my master goes," said I; as he leapt out of the window into the orchard below. Behind the haystacks in the hotel's compound, we hid ourselves. Barely two minutes after that an English detachment, following the Indians, was searching the hotel for fleeing Turkish soldiers.

'Never was there to be greater tension in my life than when I was lying, covered in hay below that hotel window, waiting to be stuck through by a probing bayonet.

'After what seemed an age, I heard an English soldier say to his officer: "I smell them Turks yet, sir."

'What a relief when his officer only laughed at the remark. The thought in my mind was that perhaps he knew a Turk might be nearby: but would never run far, no matter from whom.

'It was well past midnight by the time that the whole of that Syrian town slumbered – the prize of an English victory: then the hero of the Turks and I moved out of our hiding places. Now, disguised by our Sufi allies as wandering Dervishes, we were escorted safely out of the city as part of a band of itinerant friars.

'Dawn found us again in our own Turkish camp, and those who were anxious lest the Ghazi had been captured by the Western Allies came in groups to see for themselves that we were alive.

'Then the hour struck for the victory of Kemal; although denounced as a rebel by his colleagues in Constantinople, he rallied the soldiers of the Sultan in Anatolia under his banner.

'It was at Samsun, where he landed, ostensibly to disarm his forces, but in reality to project a new plan for Turkey to bring it out of the slough of the Sultan's time: there I saw the real Kemal. The scene in that small schoolroom in which he addressed his followers is sharp in my memory.

'"Men of my race," rose his voice, "death comes to every man and woman. Since there is no escape from it, why die like vermin? Shall we not die like Turks?"

'The atmosphere was electric, and not only metaphorically, for a tremendous thunderstorm was raging outside and lightning had struck an adjoining building.

'He spoke of the great sacrifices that his people had made. He recalled the great glory that was Sultan Fateh's, whose name had resounded up to the walls of Vienna: he impressed upon his hearers that the bullets of the enemy had never deflected an attack of the Turkish nation.

'"And are we not that same nation still?" he roared, his face flushed with excitement. He held up the Sultan's telegram making peace – saying: "If there ever was a mere scrap of paper, it is this, it is this, it is this; the Sultan selling us to our enemies."

'Within twenty days, ragged and ill-fed men from the deserts of the east, from the uplands of Turkish Kurdistan, from the pasture lands of Kasysari, swelled his ranks and turned into a mighty army. That starving, supposedly defeated rabble not only redeemed the national sovereignty of the Turks, but it showed the world once again that one man alone could still make a dismembered people form a solid unit.

'That he, although defeated on all fronts during the Great War, pronounced a rebel, both against the Sultan's State and the Moslem faith by the Grand Mufti of Constantinople, could not only muster an effective force for resistance, but could actually smash the mighty army of Greece, and win back a place for his people in the first rank of the community of nations: that is so much recent history, which I do not need to repeat.

'This solid fact is a tribute to this wondrous man, this one man, who is the New Turkey personified.

'"Now what are you going to do about the veiling of women?" asked a Deputy from a remote, conservative town. Kemal looked hard at the man, and asked a coffee-vendor to give some more coffee to the interrogator.

'"Drink another cup, my friend," said the Ghazi to the man, "to help you to recollect that the days of the Sultans are over. We are living in a new age, with new ideas, new ideals."

'An ink-bottle was standing on the desk beside me; and, as he picked it up, I hoped that he would not throw it at the Deputy in his rage; but instead, placing a sheet of paper on it, he tied a string over the stopper. Then he addressed us all.

'"You see that bottle wrapped in paper? Well, our women were clothed in their veils and trailing costumes, covered from head to foot like this bottle. Fresh air could not get to their lungs, they could not exercise their limbs, and piled on fat lolling upon cushions."

'With a sneer he looked at the Deputy who disliked the unveiling.

'"And you, you would like the women to be like fat cows, I suppose? No, we need women who can stand shoulder-to-shoulder with men in all walks of life. We do not want to bury half the Turkish population in sloth and treat them as pieces of furniture."

'And sure enough it was so, too, for the next day when I wanted to make a long journey into the interior of Anatolia, it was a young girl of the new Turkey who mapped out my route, standing behind the counter unveiled like any other European woman.

'For some months after the convocation of the National Assembly, it was part of my duty to go to Izmir, until a telegram from Ankara summoned me to the new capital.

'Taking advantage of the Ghazi's illness some of the Deputies had hatched a plot against him in the National Assembly. It was planned that next time he would not be elected President.

'Ankara could not have seen a greater deluge of rain during its hoary history than the one we were experiencing as we – some of the Old Guard – padded our way to the Parliament building.

'The Ghazi was so ill that his doctors had forbidden him to attend the election; and the speeches which his opponents made on that occasion left none in doubt that whoever might be elected president, at least for them the Great Hero was not in the running.

'When the time for the final vote came we could scarcely believe our eyes as we watched Kemal being lowered into his chair in the President's Gallery from a stretcher.

'He had come to address the House, "at least once more before I die", someone heard him say.

'As he staggered up to speak, the crowded House was hushed to silence, an ominous silence, such as descends upon frightened birds before a storm bursts.

'He addressed us till long after midnight, fainted, then revived, stood up and told us that he cared nothing for himself, but only for the nation. In the cause of the people he justified certain laws, and begged his hearers to act wisely.

'The Turks are, in many ways, honest and simple like children. When they saw and heard this man, their emblem of regeneration, then without exception everyone wept, wept too with the thought of the great services this one man had rendered them. He was re-elected unanimously, and borne to his residence in royal state as dawn was breaking over the distant ruined walls that still skirt old Ankara.

'"I am not happy in this ancient dwelling," he once remarked to me as we watched the Turkish fleet pass before us at Istanbul. He was never happy in the palaces of the Sultans.

'Then, one day, I saw him in his new home in Chinkaya Hills overlooking the gorgeous lowlands that kiss the Angorian Ranges.

'At a distance of even ten yards you would hardly notice the house, for curiously it is built in the old English baronial style. The same sort of turrets, the same kind of walls, only orientalized; and a vast green lawn, very much like an English bowling-green, surrounds it. Kemal loved to bask in the sun on that lawn.

'Every day after his breakfast of dry toast, some milk and many cigarettes, you could see him walking bareheaded, with a little bald patch showing on his crown, walking deep in thought, and never without a cigarette.

'Both at lunch and at dinner, when he invited a few of his old comrades, I always left the table with my appetite only half-satisfied. At midday, little was served besides soup, salads, rice, fruit and cheese. Dinner, too, would not boast more than four courses, though of course, there was always a box of cigarettes in front of him. At times he was entirely enveloped in smoke. Although reputed to drink alcohol, I never saw him take wine.

'Whenever it was my good fortune to work there, I found that practically every paper in the files which I had left for his orders, was read and even corrected, for Kemal worked with astonishing rapidity. Give him a book and he would finish it at one sitting – that is, if he liked the book. Particularly, he liked to read the biographies of great men – his knowledge of Napoleon was vast. He even recited some of his poems to us; and his compositions were often much better than those of many modern poets in Turkey.

'Another remarkable thing about him, almost approaching fastidiousness, concerned the neatness of his appearance and dress. He would not wear the same shirt two days running, nor go out of his bedroom without first oiling and mastering his hair.

'It is the latter facet of his personality which may have attracted his wife – the beautiful daughter of a wealthy merchant in Izmir. And when Kemal decided upon a course of action, what he resolved had to be done.

'I well remember an occasion when in a brusque manner, he scolded me by saying: "Do you know the difference between a great man and one like you? It is," he enlightened me, "that one makes up his mind about a thing and does it irrespective of consequences while the other dilly-dallies and loses. If you had done the former," he smiled that smile so full of meaning, "you would have become President of the Turkish Republic in place of me."

'This shows that Kemal was not really vain, but had an extraordinary amount of self-confidence. Maybe it was that tremendous will that clashed with the will of his wife: one day we saw the lady leave for her father's home and she never returned as the President's wife to Ankara.

'I knew and studied him for years and yet I must own that I did not really know him at all; how much did anyone know of Kitchener, of Bismarck or of Napoleon? The actual characteristics of such men are not readily unveiled. What can one "know" of a man who speaks perhaps a hundred words a day, and sits mute as a Buddha, surrounded by clouds of cigarette smoke?

'Some will tell you that Kemal was a mechanical organizer whose mentality ran on the wheels of system alone; others, that he was an inspired patriot, so absorbed in the task of nation-building that he had no time nor thought for anything else. From what I know of him there is a modicum of truth in both opinions.'

The air was crisp with the early morning mist as I sallied forth to make a round of the old town of Ankara. I was not as early as I had thought. Climbing those inclines that take one right into the heart of the town where the old Turkey can still be seen, I found women already going about their business.

They were as covered by their cloaks as any woman one might see in Central Asia or Afghanistan. The Law of the Ghazi says that the women should unveil themselves, but the older generation cannot adapt to the new conditions.

Around the pump in the middle of a square up the hill, I

saw girls of ten and fourteen filling their pitchers; smaller ones ran in and out of the adjoining houses playfully engaged in early morning shopping. Yes, shopping, because nearby a man was selling hot buns for breakfast.

Turkish workmen, looking brisk and alert, carrying the tools of carpentry or those used in masonry, were emerging from their houses – houses that still retained their ancient character, with a high wall surrounding them, and windows that did not open onto the street. Suddenly there was a twitter amongst the urchins. A Moslem priest dressed in his long flowing garb, had come upon the scene and was marshalling the members of his street-school into some kind of order.

What with the excitement of seeing the schoolmaster and protests against my taking her photograph, a pretty little girl dropped her copper water-bowl.

Picking it up hurriedly, she wiped it with the end of her headscarf.

'May Allah forgive thee,' she lisped innocently, 'there are verses of the Koran inscribed on this bowl, and the Holy Words have touched the ground – fallen even where my feet are.'

That little remark, more than anything else throughout my wanderings in modernist Turkey, convinced me that Islam had very deep roots in the hearts of the Turkish people, long before the resurgence of fundamentalism.

Nor, indeed, could Islam be long divorced from their minds, because for more years than many other Moslem empires, these Turks had been the custodians of a powerful Islamic heritage. The pendulum has swung back with a vengeance within fifty years of the 'dethronement of Allah', as Western so-called analysts called it. Today, Islam is a powerful force in Turkey, and no politician can afford to disregard it.

But people listened to the intellectuals – never a good idea – and not to a little girl. She had addressed me barely two hundred yards from that part of Ankara where the foreigner, sitting in the sumptuously-decorated lounge of a hotel, would hear from some youth of Turkey that he, at least, does not believe in Allah.

Early during my first visit to the Republic, I was at the foot of the hill where the President was to review his troops towards noon. As such ceremonials go, it might not excel the wonderful spectacle seen on a similar occasion in London; but it was at least symbolic of the fact that 'the Great Father was reviewing his children', as they termed it in Turkey. It certainly was Kemal who shaped the army of modern Turkey, and still cherished it as the surest bulwark of the independence of his country.

There was the usual march-past, the cavalry, the infantry, the gunners and even the nursing corps – all were there; all saluted, bands played, orders were shouted; and it was over in just under an hour, after which the Ghazi sat down to lunch with his officers in a field camp.

But the true index of all this preparedness was the reception by the public. Directly after lunch, when the gun boomed out the news that the President was on his way to his palace at Chinkaya Hill and would be passing through the town, I was there at a window to witness the scene.

Pavements were lined with men and women; windows of houses and shops were a sea of faces; there was a tense silence, then the distant roar of cheers struck upon the ear. The cavalcade had started.

Nearer and nearer sounded the cheering. I left the

window, as I wanted to watch the reaction of the people from a place where I could be closer to them.

The crowd now surged like a whirlpool. People had invaded the road itself. There was hardly ten feet of room left in the middle for the passage of the President's car; and now the suppressed emotion let itself go, because the outriders could be seen thundering up Karaoghlu Street, past the offices of the ministries.

Cavalrymen came up two by two, then three cars followed, and then a giant of a motor-car, wherein sat the Ghazi – President Ataturk – the hero himself.

There was no holding the passion of the populace. They were shouting, yelling in Turkish, in Arabic, in Kurdish, in all the tongues known to the Middle East. They were waving flags, they were even playing the national anthem on portable gramophones. 'Our Ghazi – our deliverer – our hero,' they shouted. The enthusiasm was overwhelming.

A man with a deep scar upon his face was in tears. 'I was with this man at Gallipoli, and I know how he saved us from slavery,' he muttered, as the great car moved slowly through the crowd.

And the Ghazi Ataturk sat there smiling back his acknowledgement to his people. His face, I thought, was lit with a strange exaltation. Little wonder, too, for modern Turkey, or, indeed, the Turkish State of any sort that you might like to name, was redeemed by none other than this man. I had no illusions about it; as I walked back to my hotel I honestly felt that I had seen the Napoleon of modern times.

In making preparations to leave for the interior of southern Anatolia, I was greatly assisted by friends who were Turkish officials and who provided me with letters of introduction to various governors on my way to Syria.

The town of Adana was one which I particularly wanted to see, for there, more than in any other place, might be found the cradle of the modern Turk. Time has brought little change to it.

'At Adana, stay at Madame Subhan's,' an official counselled me. 'And do not stay in any other boarding house,' he warned, 'for they are dreadful – and may be operated by people of whom we do not approve.'

But I had been tipped off that this lady's house, though impeccably clean, was plentifully supplied with a different bug, of an electronic kind, by courtesy of the political police. Not that they had anything against me; indeed, that was, I heard, part of their problem. 'What is this man up to?' were the final words of a report, leaked to me by a Sufi who worked in the Ministry of the Interior.

I could hardly come clean on that one; certainly not at that time. The so-called Sufi Orders, mere collections of adventurers and exploiting cultists for the most part, had been suppressed by the republican authorities. Their meeting-halls were closed down and confiscated.

As someone with Sufic connections, I would soon find myself in prison together with others – such as religious fanatics and swindlers – if my cover, thin enough as an eccentric traveller, were blown.

So, of course, in spite of kindly official help, 'to smooth your way, Bayim,' I resolved to avoid Madame Subhan.

The next day I left for Konia.

Away in the province of Konia, the true Osmanli Islam still survives. Konia is a land of cornfields and pastures. Here dwelt the Seljuk Turks whose heritage helped to make the area the centre of Islamic culture for five hundred years.

In the centre of the town of Konia there is a statue of Mustafa Kemal. The hand of the statue is outstretched; beckoning the people to a further vision.

At that moment the hand of the reformer was still, and Konia was much as it was centuries ago. The winding lanes of the town were wide and clean. Every house was surrounded by high walls of clay. There were but few women in evidence, and the fez was still there. Western clothes would have created a riot.

The centre of the town was the *caravanserai* – the rest-house, where caravans assembled for and from all parts of the East.

Here traders would unload their goods and chant their prayers in gratitude for a safe journey, from behind their bales of merchandise.

The men had spread their bedding as close as possible to their camels. They squatted and inhaled the perfumed smoke from their water-pipes. One heard the Turkic speech of Samarkand, of Kirghizia, that of Kurdish Iraq, of far-off Afghanistan.

As the evening shades crept over the scene, the minarets and mosques emerged clearly from the haze of the day.

The prayer leaders intoned the evening prayers. The camels expelled and regurgitated the slimy red water-bladders from their throats.

There was one incongruous note – a rich travelling Khan had obtained a new and wondrous toy. It was a wheezy, wind-up portable gramophone. The strains of a Scottish dirge came throbbing forth. Set in a minor key, the lament added to the weirdness of the occasion.

With the coming of the dawn the atmosphere of the setting changed. The high element of business entered. Pariah dogs, tolerated until then, were kicked into the distance. Small boys, suspiciously near laboriously transported merchandise, were cuffed.

Carpets were spread. Merchants conjured up an ingratiating smile. They combed their beards, relit their pipes and saw to the braziers for the coffee-pots. The scene was set for bargaining.

Around the merchants clustered the almost-learned: the public letter-writers. They squatted on the ground with pen and ink-horn. They would inscribe letters, even compose them, at a penny a page.

They pen the Arabic characters, beginning on the right of the page and working to the left. Though the Latin alphabet is now in official use everywhere, many still prefer where possible to read or write in the Arabic script. It is quicker to use, if you are literate. It is also the lettering of the Holy Book.

'Slowly, slowly,' the scribe would reprimand an impatient merchant anxious to make out a bill. Small boys rushed up to a traveller from another Eastern country, just to show that they could still write Arabic letters – and expected no reward for it.

And the fortune-tellers! They plied a profitable trade. Merchants consulted them before embarking upon the perils of the homeward journey.

They would take the hand and place on it a pinch of red sand, allowing it to trickle slowly away. Fingering their rosary beads, they calculated mutteringly, pulling at their beards. They are great readers of character, if nothing else.

The brass fortune-telling bowl is brought out; inscribed with mystic words, it is almost an object of veneration.

Some are really ancient, but it is their inner virtue that counts.

Many swear that they have attained their heart's desire merely through drinking water swirled three times in such bowls. Some of them are tinned, to prevent verdegris, so that eating food from them can bring fortune in safety.

Here in Konia is what many consider one of the great shrines of Islam – the tomb of Hazrat Mevlana: Jalaluddin Rumi, the great Sufi poet and master, who died in the thirteenth century of the Christian Era.

Within this sacred shrine, one still finds the 'whirlers' known in the West as the Dancing Dervishes. Every Friday these Dervishes, assemble in the Hall of Music.

This is not a *dancing-hall*: its name means the Hall of Hearing, and for a very good reason which is not widely known.

According to his own writings, the spiritual teacher, Rumi of Balkh in Afghanistan established these whirling exercises 'to stir the blood of the phlegmatic Greeks': and not to produce inner results in the dervishes themselves, let alone non-Greeks.

It is the audience and not the whirlers who are to be affected, and supposed to be influenced, by the flute and the kaleidoscope of the whirling skirts.

Many people, both in the East and West, have tried to imitate the turning as a means of attaining mystical states; having forgotten the original intention, in which the dervishes were the implements enabling others to enter the spiritual condition.

So little known is this fact today that even the contemporary participants have forgotten it. They also have imitators in the West who dress up in tall hats and cloaks and try to whirl, to become attuned with the Infinite . . .

I attended a session of the 'whirlers' held, somewhat

bizarrely, under the aegis of the Turkish National Tourist Office. Officials there, I learnt, had become convinced that this 'order' could not be as harmful as others since it was admired in the West: and, in that first flush of modernisation, the West could, for the revolutionaries, do no wrong.

The dervishes held their arms aloft and whirled, supposedly in ecstasy, to the rhythmic music of the flute and the soft tantalizing roll of tiny drums. The 'voice' of the drums rapped out the words of the original poems composed by the Saint, author of the Meaningful Couplets, in Persian.

Round and round whirled the dervishes, the drums setting a maddening tempo. Faster, faster and yet faster, until the pace became delirious, these men maintained this amazing gyration, one palm upward, the other down, for some twenty minutes. Then they sank quivering to the ground. Spectators are often amazed at the performance: but it is merely the result of many months of training, with the foot revolving around a large nail hammered upright on the floor.

The flutes and drums ceased their cadences. Outside the shrine, low, set voices pitched in a minor key took up the recitation of the prayers.

Within the shrine, in a perfect state of preservation, I saw more than a thousand manuscripts. Among them were books, in classical Persian and Arabic, believed to have been used by the sainted Mevlana ('Our Lord') himself more than seven hundred years ago. They lay exactly, it is said, as he left them, open at the very page.

This fact, and some others, made me realise that I had an uphill task on my hands if I were to carry out a duty relating to this shrine which had been laid upon me.

I was welcomed with expressions of delight and every

courtesy, as I presented a letter of introduction from the world centre of the Sufis for whom I was carrying messages. As a lay messenger, I was on what is known in the East as an inspection-tour.

When I showed the Sheikh that I knew the sign-language of the dervishes and could answer test questions, all were overjoyed. They regarded me, in their own parlance, as 'a High Initiate', though among real Sufis no such thing exists: 'Either you know or you do not'.

Greeted by everyone as *Buyuk Mufetesh Efendi*, Great Mr Supervisor, I was invited to a massive feast. There an address was inscribed and entrusted to me for the head of the Sufis.

Then came the dénouement. My instructions were to break it to the Konia people that although they constantly complained of being reduced to a tourist spectacle by the Republic, this was indeed no more and no less than what they are.

There was no spiritual content in their activities, neither in the music nor the dance. I had to remind them, and was able to show them quoting chapter and verse in Rumi's own works, of the local and limited nature of the 'dance'.

I had to prove, by reference to published authoritative Sufi works, that the whirling was not for the participants at all. It was for the benefit of, and limited to, a specific audience.

Indeed, public displays had always been allowed, and all audience-halls had public galleries: centuries before the republic and the dethronement of religion in Turkey. It was intended that the 'dance' be a public spectacle.

This was, in fact, only what the supposedly enlightened dervishes, so often likened to monks, were still doing. This, then, and much else, I laboriously explained. The dervishes' faces hardened more and more with every sentence I spoke, and some were even making threatening gestures, shaking their clenched fists in the air, in a most unspiritual way.

Eventually the old Chelebi Sheikh, 'Head of the Order' as he was known, dismissed the members of his community and invited me to confer with him alone.

When we were seated in his private cell, he said: 'My son, this is the year thirteen forty-nine [of the Islamic Era]: you are young, and you are of course only doing your duty. Dervishes, I do know now, are not mystics but those *striving* for spiritual insight: and that is what we are.

'We are devout, though not illuminated. But people in general do not know this. We can perhaps give them a taste, if not any knowledge . . .

'We are not Sufis, who are the already-enlightened ones. So we must defer to the knowledge of the Sufis who sent you.

'They know what we do not. But we can say that we represent devotion without having it, like an emblem or symbol might. In a world where there is no light at all, even a false gleam is perhaps something to have.

'At the same time I agree that we have not, as you have shown us, even studied our First Teacher's words well enough to know that this whirling is for Sufis to control, and not for us to benefit from.

'But I am old, and set in my ways. I have been here so long, and so have my ancestors, that we cannot change.

'I have realised, as you were talking just now, that the spiritual life deteriorates in quality over the centuries as much as the political life: we need our own reformation, just as Turkey needed its revolution.

'But I feel happier when I whirl. Do you blame me if I thought that this was religious ecstasy? Would you yourself have known better, had you not been told by those who know better than you or I?

'Further,' – and here the old reprobate lost my goodwill as he flashed me a cunning smile – '*we* may well be wanted, and believed to be the possessors of secrets long after you and yours have passed away!

'If the Sufis who employ you will always be there, have they no mercy on a small band of luckless seekers who only want to carry on a tradition?'

I felt myself bound to say, 'But what about deceit? There are people all over the world who think you are genuine, who follow your whirling, who think that that will bring them enlightenment . . .?'

He put his hand on my shoulder. 'The whole world, friend, is deceit; everything but God is deceit, an illusion – do you presume to judge your fellow men, or what?'

'I am passing on a message', I said, huffily.

'And you have done so. I am sure that you were not also instructed to enter into a debate with me. I shall bear witness, if necessary, that you have given me the message, and that is enough, is it not?'

I had to concur with his rhetorical question. Then he twisted the knife in the wound.

'We are here, after seven hundred years, not because of our value or viciousness, but because people *want* us. They want magic. Few are chosen to become Sufis; many can follow a harmless path and feel better, elevated. That, in any case, is what they imagine spirituality to be.'

Though scandalised, I summoned what gravitas I could, and bade this semi-charlatan farewell. He and all his band gave me a cordial send-off. The old fellow assembled as many of the local populace as he could, to show them how honoured he and his crew were in foreign lands . . .

Not a single one of the dervishes, whether young or old, seemed in the slightest undermined by my news . . .

Sixty years on, the old Sheikh's words have been proved to be true. He is dead, but people still follow the Whirling Path . . .

Who am I to judge? Nobody. Nor do I – I merely report.

Travelling further afield, to the southern confines of the Turkish Republic, I arrived at Adana to hear, as I had been promised by a historian, a story of life in a Sultan's harem, at first-hand.

Many sensational tales of life in the *seraglio* had been published in the West. People were beginning to suggest that these were just the result of an overheated imagination combined with the repressions of the Victorian age.

But I was to find some confirmation, at least, of the lurid legends . . .

In Adana I found lodging, not with Madame Subhan, but in the house of Kasima. She was a grey-haired Circassian lady of remarkable dignity and, despite her years, of erect and dignified carriage. In earlier years she had lived in the *seraglio*.

Like Zobeda, Kasima was timid at first. Many years of incarceration behind the walls of the Sultan's seraglio had rendered her fearful of meeting the world. Ingrained in her mind was a fear of the opposite sex.

With a man in close proximity, she saw not an ordinary male being but the bastinado and the other instruments of correction maintained by the chief eunuch for those women of the harem who might momentarily forget that they were the slaves of the Sultan.

Many decades had passed since Turkey's Sultan had fled precipitately before the advancing forces of the battle-scarred general to be known as Mustafa Ataturk, Father of the Turks, but in thought Kasima still dwelt within the harem.

It took me a long time to gain her confidence, and still longer to break down the barriers of reserve built up by a long-regimented discipline.

At length, she consented to tell me of her life behind the high and impenetrable walls of the last of the great harems.

In doing so she broke vows of horrific import, and it required a supreme effort of will on her part to realize how many years had flown since she passed from the malignant care of the eunuchs.

In her mind's eye, she could still see the bared scimitars and the weighted sacks believed always to be ready to receive any fair denizen of the harem who had so much as been suspected of whispering its secrets. Only the Sultans know how many young women were drowned in the Bosphorus because of the tittle-tattling of some disgruntled eunuch.

Kasima's story is thus probably unique, for few have dared to speak of the harem except in the abstract, and it is unlikely that any harem woman ever before has delivered herself of such intriguing reminiscences.

As she wove a pattern of intrigue, hate, passion and unrivalled luxury, I gradually realized that I was listening not to polite conversation but rather to a piece of history. On later reflection, I felt it almost a duty to preserve her story, and commit it to writing as a historical document of the late nineteenth and early twentieth centuries at the Sultan's court.

I had entertained an entirely erroneous idea of a Sultan's harem; and yet I imagine that my impression was and still is generally and widely held. So inviolable has been the secrecy which cloaked the private lives of the Sultans that an imperfect picture was bound to arise in the minds of outsiders.

To me, the harem had been a huge palace replete with every feminine luxury, in which were congregated numbers of beautiful women, all highly perfumed, all attired in priceless silks, all mistresses of coquetry, and all only awaiting the pleasure of their royal master.

Kasima speedily dispelled this picture.

She told me a loosely-woven story of her parents – they were peasants, and very poor. She remembered with a vague pride that she was the youthful belle of her hamlet – for girls come to maturity quickly in the hills of Circassia.

There had been the shy, sheeplike glances of the youths, and the more direct ogling of the older men. Because once she had smiled at an audacious sally, her father had beaten her.

As in the case of many other young girls in Georgia, her parents had certain plans for her when she was old enough. Her mother had wept, it was true, when the time came, but then there was the inevitable long journey in a rough, springless cart drawn by two white, long-horned oxen, and then – the sale.

Dimly she recalled her first reactions to her lot. When her father bade her farewell she cried, even though he had beaten her.

Roughly he had said that she had no cause for tears, for was she not lucky, and favoured above all other girls? Had not the stars been smiling on her when her fair skin had been espied by no less a one than the Sultan's slave-agent?

Was she not herself now a bright star of the firmament, since inspection had already shown her form to be exquisite and worthy of royal attention?

She had drawn back from her father, terror-struck at his

words. Into the Circassian hills, there had for centuries percolated stories of the Sultan's harem in Istanbul, and they were not nice.

It was said that, for the slightest misdemeanour, girls were handed over to the executioner to be flung into the Bosphorus; that the soles of their feet were bastinadoed on the smallest pretext; that one's every action was spied upon by gigantic eunuchs: in a word, that the walls of the palace were those of a gilded prison, from which no inmate ever escaped except through death.

These were stories built upon centuries of rumour and innuendo. It was widely believed, for instance, that the Sultans were men whose appetite for feminine beauty was insatiable, and that this appetite was inflamed almost to the degree of imbecility. This widely-believed story had some basis in fact, for more than one Sultan was kept in feminine subjection by such dubious means.

In such cases, it was the monarch's own mother who connived at this state of affairs, for in the harem she was pre-eminent and set above all other women. With a son rendered weak and unstable by vice and continued excess, power naturally passed into the hands of the mother. She kept it firmly there.

There was, for instance, the case of Murad III, who gathered together a harem so numerous that even Solomon would have been bemused.

Murad III fathered one hundred and three children, according to the palace records, and an unknown number with temporary consorts who did not warrant the dignity of an official record.

When this Sultan died, there were twenty sons and twenty-seven daughters still living – the remainder having died mysteriously.

The eldest son of the twenty – later to be known as

Muhammed III – put the other nineteen to death in order to make certain that none of his brothers should make a bid for the throne.

Then to make doubly sure that there should be no future male claimants, he rounded up those seven of his father's concubines who had been declared pregnant, and had them sewn up in weighted sacks. At dead of night they were thrown into the Sea.

This was the reputed atmosphere into which Kasima was so suddenly to be plunged. Little wonder that she recoiled with horror at the thought.

She saw herself in Istanbul, penned up with other recruits for the royal bedchamber. She envisaged a scene where she was bedecked with the finest raiment and ready for the dire moment of a monarch's lustful debauchery.

Vividly she conjured up hysterical scenes in the Sultan's apartments, for she resolved that she would never tamely submit her body to the attentions of such a libertine. Rather would she die . . .

How different was the reality!

Filled with the most poignant emotions, she was brought to Istanbul. She was ushered past the gigantic eunuchs on duty at the various gates and found herself, not in the role of a concubine, with a galaxy of slaves to massage and perfume her body, but a maker of coffee and, as she was speedily informed, a very indifferent one at that.

Curiously enough, this sudden tumbling of the ogre's castle of her dreams piqued her. When chided because of the noxious character of the brew she had produced in the name of mocha coffee, she turned upon her tormentor and informed her, with peasant forthrightness, that she had been brought all the way from Circassia to delight the Sultan, and not to be a menial.

The beautifully-groomed woman who was Controller of the Harem and her task-mistress, laughed loudly at this sally; then turned upon the unfortunate Kasima and berated her.

Who was she – an uncouth village jade – to aspire to such greatness? In time perhaps – when Kasima had been taught the ways of the court, when she had learned something of deportment and of court etiquette; then she might dream of such an honour.

If the stars were beneficent, she might even attain her desire, but for the moment she had to learn – she had to be trained – and her immediate task was to make coffee and – to make it well.

There was much more in the same vein and the now dignified old lady smiled faintly at the recollection of her youthful presumption.

Kasima explained further. She soon wrecked my preconceived notion of a palace peopled by idle, bored, lethargic beauties, waiting, waiting for a summons. Everyone worked.

She told me of the interior economy of the palace and she explained what a complicated institution it really was, where occupation was found for all and none was allowed to fritter away time.

The most powerful woman in the old Ottoman Empire was the Sultan's mother. Her place in the State was unique, and no mere wife or concubine of the Sultan, no matter the degree of his infatuation, could supplant her. She gave up the reins of her office only when she died.

This woman, known as the Sultana Validà or Queen Mother, ruled sternly over all others, and none could dispute her will. In the old Ottoman hierarchy, had she not been selected for the highest honour to which any person might aspire? Was she not the custodian of the monarch's most cherished treasures – not his immense wealth, or his priceless jewels, his empire even: but that which transcended all – his women?

She soon learned that it was the Sultana Validà who wielded all power within the harem, and Kasima had to shrink back against the wall and efface herself when this great lady passed, for it was she who ultimately indicated how each woman there should spend her hours, what tasks she should perform, and even what clothes she might wear.

Below the Sultana were the *kadins*, concubines who had attained the position of wives by bearing the Sultan a son. These women had magnificent apartments, and were regarded and treated as queens.

Below the *kadins* were other women who had been shown preferment – women who had attended the royal bedchamber but who had failed to provide the Sultan with offspring.

They, as some slight recompense for the dignity and the opulence which they had so narrowly missed, had been awarded appointments within the harem.

Thus there was the Controller of the Harem, the Treasurer, the Keeper of the Baths, the Mistress of the Robes, the Keeper of the Jewels, and a dozen others.

Whatever else it was or was not, the harem was the fast track to possible great power for the female in the Turkish Ottoman Empire.

And below all these, there were the newcomers like Kasima. She was attached, as an apprentice coffee-maker, to the entourage of the Controller of the Harem. There were many other girls, some under her tutelege, others under that of the Mistress of the Robes or in the service of the numerous other women principals.

All the girls were required to work really hard. Some,

like Kasima, had to learn to cook; others embroidered and stitched the fine silks which adorned the *kadins*; yet others kept in repair the priceless rugs and carpets. Some were singers, some musicians, artists, calligraphers – there was work enough for all.

You will notice in this brief sketch of the harem's interior economy that Kasima had so far not mentioned the eunuchs, except in passing. That is because these *castrati*, while of the harem, were an organization apart.

Responsible only to the Sultana was the Chief Eunuch, and though he worked under the orders of the Sultan's mother, it was ultimately he, and he alone, who was responsible for the good behaviour of the harem's inmates.

This was because, should anything untoward occur, the Sultan could hardly chide his august mother. The Chief Eunuch was there for this purpose, but his power over the girls was real and sometimes terrible.

At his service were other eunuchs – dozens of them – and they provided the secret organization which kept the Sultana acquainted with all that transpired in the harem on the one hand, and at the court of the Sultan on the other; for the Chief Eunuch had direct access to the monarch and, indeed, was his channel of communication between the throne and the concubines and concubines-to-be.

Kasima told me how the Chief Eunuch and his underlings could make or mar the life of any woman. A word whispered into the Sultan's ear, and priceless riches and the dignity of queenhood might become a girl's perquisites.

A vitriolic innuendo whispered into the Sultana's ear, and a girl was given the most menial tasks, was garbed in unattractive attire, and perhaps even beaten.

Kasima's stories amazed me. They were outrageously bizarre, yet starkly simple. They both appalled me and excited my interest for more.

But I had my own duty to perform. I had to journey southward into Syria, then under French suzerainty.

The scene changed as I jostled along on a protesting camel: from here on I was travelling with a caravan, and had discarded my European clothes.

The first thing I noticed was that the Arab women were subtly different.

Most of them, here, were unveiled. They sat, shapeless forms, perched precariously upon donkeys. Children shared their voluminous laps with the latest offspring of the family goat.

The men had clipped, short beards and longer, often hooked and Semitic-looking noses. There was a curious pinkness in their complexions that one saw all over Syria. This was due to the effect of the burning sun upon less-pigmented skins.

The camel, too, largely gave place to the dromedary.

Here there was no statue of Mustafa Kemal. Here the Hero, the Pasha, the General, the Saviour of the Nation, Father of the Turks, was but another name.

3

My Caravan in Allah's Dawn

There is magic, there is romance, in Turkey.

Syria was once part of the Empire of Turkey.

When I passed the frontier post into Syria, I seemed to lose the sense of unreality and of fantasy which still linger in the kingdom of the Sultans. Now I found myself plunged into a different sort of adventure. Dressed as one of its people, a son of Asia, and perched on the back of a camel, I felt I could view the ancient East in its true colour and beauty.

My caravan had the best part of a hundred miles of caravan route to cover before I could arrive at Aleppo. By air or car, I could have reached my journey's end much quicker and travelled in greater comfort. But I neither wanted too much comfort nor desired to reach any given region too soon. So I chose the caravan route.

And imagine our camel-train trampling a carpet of living gold all day beneath a sky of brightest turquoise! I have frequently heard men speak of the weariness of the desert, of its changelessness which breeds the discontent of satiety, as does the sea; yet I have never experienced the slightest ennui on this account. Why?

For one thing, the caravan is much too varied in its personnel and its continual diversity to make for dullness. Travelling in a caravan is like marching in a picture – a large and lustrous painting, one of those rich and rare canvasses one sees more often in public galleries than in private houses – always in the centre of the picture, at its brightest spot, and never near the edge of the frame.

All around is scattered the whole wealth and brilliance of the artist's palette – the most amazing greens from the dye-vats of Damascus, reds and scarlets which could only have come from the Bosphorus and the delicate hues of Persian prayer-rugs.

The feeling is one of having emerged from the sunrise with all its colours about you, enfolding you, drenching you – and all through the hours tramping in billows of gold-dust.

Boredom? The man who could feel bored in such a progress as this would walk disinterested through the courts and gardens of Paradise.

The progress of the caravan is as replete with surprises as is the voyage of a ship through some archipelago of the sun. Once a day at least the green islands of oases lift their coasts above the yellow waves of sand, beckoning just as do islands in the Pacific or the Caribbean. Like a ship the caravan approaches them, the leading camel with its arched neck appearing as the figurehead on the prow.

The best time to arrive at an oasis is at the hottest hour of the day, when noon is pouring down its vertical vigours. There is a sense of instant relief on entering the province of the palm, such as a man blinded by lights feels on entering a shuttered room.

Cool, green avenues shut out the blaze; friendly waters irrigate the blood and one can feel the flesh returning to its norm of temperature and ease. It is only on leaving the desert for a space that a man realises the toll which it takes of a person's physical strength, not while still drenched in its vitality.

It is the romance of cavalcade and colour which frees the traveller in the caravan from any sense of weariness. As well ask a knight in armour if he ever felt the weight of his panoply when on journey errant, or the opera star if he or she wilts from the stifling heat of the theatre, the oppression of plastered-on makeup or the arid bareness of backstage.

I was part of a pageant, of a procession, and processions never feel fatigue. I was a unit in a 'crowded hour of glorious life'.

I and my camel were one, I was a centaur of the desert; or a man stalking upon the shoulders of a great beast to nowhere or somewhere, and I did not care when I arrived or if I never arrived at all. The whole business began to take on the feeling and appearance of a golden dream, in which the elements were a yellow carpet, an azure canopy, splashes of rainbow colours and the smell of camels.

It was one of those dreams of which the actuality is more gallant and desirable, more marvellous and satisfying, than any memory of it.

Day after day we rode on, or marched beside our camels, singing desert songs, kneeling in prayer five times a day, and at the close of the day going to bed either in a serai, or on a mattress of soft sand under the roof that Allah made.

We stayed in one caravanserai – a resthouse – not very far from Aleppo. A walled quadrangle it was, where the men and beasts of our caravan entered for a night's rest. Around the walls, low-roofed rooms, really mere cells, were hurriedly claimed by the merchants of the caravan: the muleteers preferred to sleep in the open.

When I swept the mud floor of my cell, a mullah of Konia, who shared it with me, showed annoyance.

'Brother, you are wasting time!' He clutched me by the elbow. 'Dust is what our bodies are made of: human flesh will become dust: why, then, be so particular about touching a thing of which you must ultimately become a part!' He motioned me to stand beside him for the evening prayer.

Almost everyone had kindled a fire: we cooked dried meat mixed with millet; for our pudding, we bought dry dates from the keeper of the serai. We told each other tales from our own countries, far into the night, while the half-moon shimmered in a sapphire sky and stars seemed to hang down towards us like giant luminous bunches of enchanted grapes.

At dawn the caravan started on its way: shouts from the drivers down the long irregular line and the camels rose from their knees with the ungainly hesitation of their kind. A swirl of sand eddied away with the light morning breeze but left the picture of the slow-moving caravan unblurred.

And what a picture! There was a music in that slow and graceful motion, and as one watched it the heart framed a tune to accompany it – something like the ballet music in Schubert's 'Rosamunde', something with an *obbligato* of bells and cymbals.

I have seen plenty of screen and television pictures of caravans in motion, but I can assure you that they bear only a very faint resemblance to the actual thing.

To begin with, they are nearly always synthetic affairs, a

producer's idea of 'the Orient' and they lack the abounding sensation and fantastic emanation of the true caravan. For just as real poetry carries with it in its flow and passion, a light above the line, which is not to be found in that which is not poetry, and is invisible to those who have not its secret, so the rich wonder and surprise of the caravan rising into motion can be comprehended only by those who have the East at heart and who understand its near-incommunicable language.

Yet not more than a few minutes ago, all this beauty was flattened to the earth, undistinguished, almost sordid in appearance. It is as though a moving flower-garden had suddenly arisen from a bed of toadstools.

This marvellous silhouette, picked out in reds, greens and blues, was squatting circles, surrounded by greasy pots, broken food and heaps of baggage. All those arching necks, that rhythmic stalking, those fluttering scarves and cloaks, where only a moment ago there was a huddle of limbs and weaving upon the desert's dusty face.

What magic has transformed it so suddenly? Surely nothing but the marvel of the kaleidoscope, which out of a few shards of coloured glass is capable of making itself over and over again into Arabian shapes and patterns of mathematical loveliness.

For there is something mathematical in all the beauty of the East: a symmetry, a blending of form, colour and something more. This endless capacity to conceive, consciously or unconsciously, design after design in recurring and orderly sequence is to be observed in the mural decoration of all Islamic lands.

So the caravan arranges and disposes itself against the desert background in a score of shifting patterns and outlines as it moves, but always flowing into set patterns, like the movement of water into pre-carved channels.

Now it appears as a long line spread across sand-hills, ghostly, spiritual; then a thickening mass of movement in some hollow, always the most material of mounted crowds, yet bearing – even in its commonplace aspect – something of that spell of the unusual which associates things Oriental with the spirit of Otherwhere.

To translate Eastern words and phrases into Western ones is only to ruin the concepts which lie in them. The phrase 'Ship of the Desert' rapidly becomes a cliché in English, not to be used because it is too familiar. But its equivalent in Arabic, *Safinat Al-Sahra*, has an enduring magic, however often it is said.

Far behind it now, the caravan has left a little knot of friends and relatives who came to see it depart. Those were waving hands, waving to speed the setting forth of a great liner; for if the camel is 'the ship of the desert', the caravan is its fleet: though I prefer the softer, Arabic word: *Al-Ustoul*.

We are away to the White City called Aleppo.

Aleppo! The name is sufficiently alluring – but how disappointing is the reality.

A dozen conquerors have ravaged the city since 854 B.C., and not so many years ago the setting was essentially Eastern. Aleppo was once one of the greatest marts in world trade. The fame of its bazaars spread even to far-off Gaul.

Now the city is a mass of architecture erected in the approved Continental European manner. Where once there were souks, there are now many shops and each displays Western wares.

There is, of course, still the ancient city, clustered around the immense Citadel. This massive structure is littered with ruins. Dogs, goats and donkeys drink from what once were ornate marble baths.

The gateway of the Citadel still stands (though within there lies a grotesque ruin). It still bears the inscription of Sultan Saladin the Great. The Syrians hastened to assure me that they would never forget that the French occupiers allowed their colonial troops to cook their meals within it.

Again and again, travelling in the East, one comes across this fierce and unforgiving attitude towards the former colonial Powers. It is something which we of the West would only have understood if the boot had been on the other foot.

Certain it is that it will not die out lightly: it was as strong in Syria in 1989 as I had heard it in 1928, sixty years before . . . Equally certainly, it is not yet understood in the West: which must, surely, put many of our calculations adrift. Islamic fundamentalism, as I was often assured by sober observers, is at least in part, one of the consequences of the colonial past.

As well as fervent nationalists, Aleppo supported a thriving community of Arab, Turkish and European self-styled dervishes. They were confused about how to recognise a true Sufi teacher, and I had been deputed to give them some indications.

Generally their imaginings – for that was all they were – centred around a kind of Indian guru-figure, a Western monk, or an Eastern dervish. All, of course, were equally far from the Sufi Arif: 'He who Knows'.

In short, they were ripe either to develop their own, emotion- and rule-based cult, or to adopt almost any ignorant, dishonest or self-deluded 'teacher' who might appear.

The 'Eleven Points' which were entrusted to me to

communicate to these good people, and to explain if I could, are listed in an Appendix at the end of this book.

From Aleppo to Antioch! The way lay through gates, under arches and upon roads built by the Romans.

Antioch, the wondrous creation of Seleucus Nicator. If this great builder returned, would he recognize his handiwork of two thousand years ago?

When I limped into the city, two donkeys were pulling a rubbish cart beside the site of the Palace of Trajan, where once tiny gold chariots, pulled by turtle-doves, carried red roses between the monarch and his queen as they feasted at their high table.

The columns of the double colonnades which long ago stood on each side of the streets lay forlorn in the dust. Some of the columns were broken and split. Others were as they had been when first they were erected.

The beautiful Orentes, with its cascades and its waterfalls, still flows and the crocuses grow wild along its banks. They peep, here and there, from some Roman sarcophagus, hundreds of which lie half-buried in the sands of time.

I wanted to wander in Antioch, so I resolved to stay in a caravanserai for a number of days and look round at my leisure.

Much had befallen here that is now history and the atmosphere had me in its spell.

4

Sons of Old Syria

Modern Antioch is comfortable enough: but, leaving it, I walked in the ancient city on the plateau of the hill where most of the famous remains lie.

The part in which I delighted particularly was the Old Wall. Commencing at the river below, it rides up to the hills and works its course on and upwards.

An earthquake in 1872 destroyed every vestige of it on the plain, but up in the hills fragments remain, looking like the scratchings on some absent-minded artist's pad and telling the tale of its glory in bygone days.

Built of limestone, its cavities are filled in with rough stones. In places – near the aqueduct for example, it may be as much as ten feet thick. At one time there were three hundred and sixty three-storied towers along it, spaced at intervals of only fifty or sixty feet, each tower rising eighty feet high.

Beginning on the western side, I saw the beautiful aqueduct bridging the valley and, following it round, I reached the Bab-al-Hadid, the Iron Gate. Near this point the wall bridges a deep valley. At the lower end it is more or less open to allow the passage of the melted waters after the winter months.

Another time, I took a road or track to a remarkable

region called the House of Water. Arriving there at mid-day, I was received in his encampment by Al Rais-an-Nour, a Sheikh of great local importance.

There I was to meet one of the most curious characters I ever knew. He was leader of the secret community called the Druse – a tall, imposing man with grey hair and blue eyes, whose people are scattered throughout the Eastern Mediterranean states.

Nobody knows their origins. They seem to be a type of Islamic Shiah, followers of Ali (the Prophet's son-in-law) whom they see as near-divine. They believe in reincarnation, as he told me, and call this transmigration *tajaiyul*, the Coming of the Jils, or generations.

The Alim or Sage as he was known, was attended by two acolytes, and treated with the greatest respect. One of their tenets is, when advisable, to be all things to all men.

As he explained when we had got to know each other, to Sunni (more orthodox) Muslims they say that they are Sunnis, while to Christians and Jews they avow those faiths, and so on.

They also believe that their hidden leader and mentor of the age lives in Europe. Our contact, set up by friends of friends of mine, had persuaded some Druses that I might be a Druse or might know something about them. Hence the Alim was prepared to talk to me.

Not, however, before he had seen me, as he requested, 'make the Sign'. This I did as coached: I prostrated myself in a certain way, and kissed the ground.

He then asked, in a peculiar voice, 'What or who is Abd-al-Nour?'

'It is the phrase, Servant of Light, used for Wine,' I answered, in the same intonation.

Now he was beaming. 'Will you share a word with me?'

'Willingly.'

'Then what comes after A?'

'M.'

And after M?

'Only S.'

This referred to the word AMS, the initials of the names of the Three Friends, Ali, Mohammed and Salman the Persian, the alleged holy trinity or very first teachers, of the Druse.

I threw in a further identity test, just for full measure, saying to the Alim:

'I have a relative and I wonder if you know him?'

'How is he styled?' asked the Alim, making a hand-signal at the same time.

'Husain,' I said, confirming the signal.

'Son of Hamdan,' continued the Sage, again with a sign.

I made the final sign in this series. 'The Khusaibi,' I ended.

He expressed himself more than satisfied; indeed, delighted: and embraced me with a powerful hug.

'Truth,' he told me, in answer to my question, 'according to our belief, is the body of man, and religion is merely the clothing. It does not matter to the body what clothes it wears.'

This is a typical example of *tawil*, interpretation (literally 'extending') whereby Islamic beliefs, for certain sectarians, can be made to mean almost anything.

All religions, said the Alim, have the same origin. They are started from the Source of Divinity, which communicates them to the Soul, the Ambassador. This Ambassador preserves the materials for the Preceeder. He or she in turn gives this to the Successor. According to the Druses, the outward form ('the clothes') of every religion is secondary and from time to time new frameworks are necessary, to reach the 'body' within.

These are the commands of the Druses:

1 Accept the current form of the faith;
2 Love the Community and serve it;
3 Shun secondary beliefs (of the 'clothing').
  Confide in none but the adept;
4 Believe in God;
5 Be of the very best morals, in life and work;
6 Know the Signs and attend the Meetings.

The Alim now recited a poem to me, said to have been composed by one Iddris, possibly the medieval founder of the sect:

'How strange, how foolish, could you but see
it, are your beliefs;
'You credit the physician who is himself sick;
'You associate with the weaver who is himself
naked.
'With the carpenter who himself has a broken
door...'

The Sheikh Rais-an-Nour regaled us with a heavy meal of camel meat cooked with coriander and wild thyme, followed by dates in honey. Afterwards, I wanted to explore the locality, and was escorted by two Bedouin warriors as guides, lent by my host: more as a sign of 'my dignity' as he put it, than for protection.

A remarkable series of waterfalls delighted the eye here. Among the rich vegetation of the hillside I saw silver threads where slender waterfalls flashed like sword-blades; further on there were gigantic falls sparkling like melted precious stones, tumbling over each other to reach the glassy water of the Orentes far beneath.

Climbing up or coming down the hillsides, I came across many sarcophagi peering out of the dust of ages. Pieces of columns could be seen here and there waiting to tell the story of Roman power and grandeur to the archaeologist – if the well-organised antiquities thieves did not get them to London or to Zurich first.

On one occasion when the Sheikh was with me, a grotto attracted my attention and, as I went to descend a long flight of stone steps, the Sheikh yelled out:

'That is the den of Satan!' and he pulled at my sleeve. 'The mother of Satan may be there even as I speak.'

He believed the local Arab legend that these caves are infested with evil spirits, and at night a light is seen to emerge from them which 'floats over the hills and the desert: and enveloping an unmarried woman would make her demented'.

The Sheikh had, it appeared, had many experiences with women. The memory of these unfortunate events clearly emphasised his belief in the influence of the grotto upon the temperament of the women of the desert.

As nothing more could be seen that day around the House of Water, I sat beside the Sheikh in his black tent while his Abyssinian slave poured water on my hands. Then rice with which largepieces of camel's meat was cooked was placed before us as our evening repast.

Afterwards, around the fire, the Sheikh engaged me in a conversation about his principal subject of concern.

'Women are evil,' he observed.

'Not all, surely!' I objected.

'Most rather than otherwise!' he insisted.

The Sheikh now turned to me meditatively.

'Tell me, traveller,' he said, 'tell me – you have been in

Britanya – is it not true that one can obtain a wife there for no more than the price of a chicken?'

I gazed at the Sheikh in astonishment.

'Is it not true,' he proceeded, noticing my air of amazement, 'that one can obtain a licence for some trifling sum, from a Government office and that thereafter one may *take* a wife?'

Enlightenment came to me.

'Not *take* a wife in the literal sense,' I was in some haste to explain. 'The marriage licence does not confer upon the Englishman the right to go into the highways and by-ways and seize any woman that attracts his eye.'

The Sheikh gave a grunt of disappointment.

'I thought it was so simple,' he said. 'I thought it was all part of this Western civilization they keep talking about, even on the radio. I have read that an Englishman pays only this small sum for his wife. And then there is the expression "taking to wife".'

With some difficulty I explained some idiosyncrasies of the English tongue. I explained that whereas in the parlance of England the man 'took' the wife, in reality it was more likely the wife who did the taking and continued to do so until she died.

'Mm-m,' he muttered, as he stroked his beard. 'Seemingly there is little difference between the desert and this wonderful London. I always knew women were evil.'

The women's liberation movement would hardly have applauded my failing to make further efforts to enlighten this gentleman. But I wonder what they would have done when faced by a dagger, a scimitar, a double-barreled shotgun and a hand-grenade? And that was only the armament on and around his person.

He was not in a good mood now.

'Take the case of that disgruntled woman,' he went on

mournfully. 'In order to get her, I had to pay her tight-fisted father three camels, fourteen goats and much silver. I heap compliments upon her and show her preference above my other wives. You can hear something of her tantrums.'

I could hear her throwing pots and pans at a woman servant, somewhere at the back of the huge tent.

'She was as sweet as bees' honey only an hour or two gone and as soft as a hovering angel. She wants one of those gold-fringed dresses which come from Damascus. The robes of my other wives are fringed with silver. I explained that were I to give her one with gold, there would be bickering and much trouble.

'Would she see reason? You observe that she would not.'

He puffed heavily on his water-pipe. 'Three camels, fourteen goats, and . . .'

He ended on this dolorous note, and lapsed into a heavy silence. Then he turned and glared at me with such a fierce look that I began to wonder whether he might not start to try out some of his implements of destruction upon me, just to relieve his feelings.

'How do you actually get your wives in the desert?' I asked in order to turn the subject.

'When a sheikh of the desert decides to take unto himself a wife,' said the Sheikh, 'he lets the fact be known.'

He continued: 'Soon he is told that there is a comely girl whose hand is ready for marriage in such-and-such a town or encampment. He is given an indication of the price he will have to pay.'

What was paid to the father of the bride was not however the total outlay. The father's share was rather in the nature of a douceur, a sort of key-money.

In addition, the intending groom had to set aside a sum

– often enormous – which was to be the wife's without a quibble in the event of divorce.

Her mother and sisters, if any, could expect to get valuable presents: which always meant gold, twenty-two or twenty-four carat, please, and plenty of it.

And then there was the expense of the wedding itself, which might put a family into debt for decades. Among the Arabs, such things are not done by halves, where the prestige of the family, or even the clan, is involved.

The Sheikh continued: 'A man might haggle over what he must pay a rapacious father, but at no time until the girl is his can he see her face. Her beauty and so on must be taken on trust.

'Sometimes the comeliness is not all that it was made out to be and the new husband feels aggrieved. Then perhaps there is born a feud of the desert which, more often than not, is wiped out in blood.' He spoke of his duel with a rival sheikh which began thus.

'There is not much romance in this, you might say.' He eyed me. 'Well, Allah knows there is not. Sometimes, however, romance comes into these affairs with the dash and flashing of scimitars, and the chivalry of our early history is reborn.

Sometimes it came in other ways. 'These young women of the desert, especially those of surpassing beauty, whose fathers have settled in the cities, have been known to gaze from a lace-thin marble window when a brave young sheikh of the desert has been passing. They have shrunk back in horror when masculine eyes have gazed into theirs and had more than a momentary glimpse of their beauty. Such was the case with my friend, Sheikh al Arabi.

'He dwells not far from Aleppo, and this happened to him, and the fire of longing raged within his heart.

'Often he passed that window again, but the young lady

knew well how she should play her part. Oftentimes he heard her singing and playing upon the stringed instruments of the harem, but he was denied any further sight of her.

'Of course, he made inquiries, but his quest seemed hopeless. Because of her beauty, he was informed, the girl had been sought by suitors from far and wide. She was actually destined for a rich old oil-sheikh who had outbid his competitors and who already had a plethora of wives.

'This was too much for my friend Al Arabi.

'One night when there was no moon, a string of the famous pure white Syrian racing camels appeared beneath the loved one's window. The Sheikh, with the aid of a ladder made from a leaning palm, made the perilous ascent. Curiously enough, the window was open.

'The girl, asleep upon her couch, shrank back in alarm when his touch awakened her, but she did not scream.

'There was the semblance of a struggle but, Allah be my witness, as my friend told me the story, I reflected that it could not have been any serious resistance which the maiden offered, for the descent of that crazy ladder was accomplished in safety.

'The champion camels did the rest. In spite of the alarm raised by the servants, and an unusually hot pursuit, the pair were soon safe away in the vast confines of the desert.

'And a happy union it proved to be, even though the young Sheikh, honourable man that he was, practically beggared himself over a period of years in order to pay the dowry.

'He stole the girl of his dreams, but no one was going to say that he was a thief, or that he stole because he could not obtain a wife by more accepted means.

'Often the desert wives gravitate to the realm of matrimony through the channels of the slave-markets which are still held in various parts of the hinterland. My best wife, who was my first love, was a slave-girl – a Kurdish girl – may Allah reward her with his best palace in Paradise, for she was the mother of my heir.'

Women *all* evil? The Sheikh had undermined his own opinions from his own mouth, I thought. Still, eyeing the armamentarium of my friend, and remembering the obligations of guesthood, I said no more on the matter, and merely thanked him for his hospitality.

Continuing my journey back to Antioch, and thence due east, striking through a chains of hills, I arrived at the village of Harim: a place straight out of the *Arabian Nights*.

Perched on the crest of a hill is a castle of surpassing beauty – chambers opening into chambers, rock-hewn stairs appearing in unexpected places: Into the mind's eye, there come flooding those old pictures of the pageantry of the Crusades.

When the great warrior monarch Nuruddin defeated the Franks here over seven centuries ago, the fort must have been a place of great magnificence. It soon fell into disrepair and, in the thirteenth century, Malik Aziz rebuilt it. His encouragement for agricultural enterprise in this region was so great that the irrigated and pampered soil is said to have rivalled that of Damascus.

On the hillside, my attention was drawn to a rock tomb. Seeing the red flags fluttering around it, 'A saint's shrine?' I asked my guide – young Sheikh Abdullah, son of Faruk.

'Nay! Allah protect us. It's no saint, but the Contractor!'

'A contractor?' I asked, bewildered.

'Yes! Baba Dost, the building contractor, who is said to have taken on the work of erecting a beautiful palace for Malik Aziz: only he could not do it. See, there is the rock throne of Dost, near his grave!' He pointed to it.

'Then why those red flags which flutter in the breeze near the tomb?' I asked.

'Because, if you repeat a story long enough many will consider it the truth! People around here are like that: and they consider the Contractor's tomb to be a shrine. Formerly they regarded him as something of a martyr at the hands of the monarch!' was the Sheikh's explanation.

'We call it a story; but it may well be true,' continued the Sheikh; when we returned to his tent. His wife, from behind the curtain, shouted:

'Abdullah, tell the traveller the story of the martyr! Tell him! Or . . .,' She threatened to relate it herself. Only that morning she had placed offerings at the shrine of Baba Dost, wishing to be vouchsafed a son. She had three daughters, and in the desert, daughters are a problem.

Laughing, the Sheikh started to tell me the story. 'Baba Dost, the Royal Contractor,' he began, 'was petrified with fright, so my mother told me, because he had been summoned to the Imperial Palace at Damascus for an audience with the Emperor Aziz, whose servant he was.

'Two years before, he had obeyed a similar summons: and the Emperor, waving a Royal arm, had commanded him to build a palace better than the red sandstone one at Damascus.

'Baba Dost, nothing loath, for he was a great builder, accepted the Royal order and had drawn heavily on the Treasury ever since. But he had been remiss, and had dallied in his work to such an extent that the palace was not built, nor even started.

71

'The Emperor ventured forth but seldom; for he loved playing chess more than going out. Meantime, Baba Dost dug ever more deeply into the Royal coffers, and had spent the money on idle diversions.

'The Emperor, for his part, accepted his assurances that all was proceeding according to plan and that a palace, far better than the one in his capital, was nearing completion. The Contractor had undertaken to finish the work in two years, and now the time was up.

'He had been summoned to give an account of his stewardship and, as he gazed round the palace, he sweated. Why had he contracted to build anything at all, much less something better than the magnificence which he now beheld!

'He stood at the centre of the inner court, beside a small channel about six inches wide. Beyond that the Emperor sat, dispensing justice, and beyond the channel none might go unbidden, not even ambassadors.

'When, in obedience to the Royal command, he had presented himself at the entrance to the audience chamber, the officer standing on the farther side of the channel called out his name to the Grand Vizir: The Grand Vizir, standing near the Emperor, informed Aziz of his presence. Aziz did not appear to hear, but that was usual. After an interval the Emperor raised his eyes, and glancing in the direction of Baba Dost, intimated to the Vizir that the Contractor might approach.

'Baba Dost advanced falteringly beneath the great awnings of red velvet, heavily embroidered with gold and supported by golden poles as thick as a man's thigh.

'Malik Aziz was reclining upon his throne. Six slaves with fans of peacocks' tails were fanning their august master. Each one of them assiduously chewed dried aromatic roots for the double purpose of reddening his lips and sweetening his breath in order that it might not offend the Emperor.

'Baba Dost glanced round the audience chamber, and shuddered. A voice came to him, whispering, yet insistent. "Better than this," it said, "Better than this!"

'He almost stumbled as the full realization of his folly came to him. He was allowed to approach to within twenty feet of the throne, but Aziz ignored his presence. Baba Dost had plenty of opportunity to take in the details of what he should have surpassed.

'The throne was about six feet long, and four wide. It had four feet, in the form of lions' paws, each massive and about twenty-five inches high. To the four feet were attached bars which supported the long seat of the throne and the twelve golden columns for the canopy.

'The feet, the bars and the columns were covered with silver inlay enriched with diamonds and rubies. In the middle of each bar was a gigantic ruby with four emeralds around it, forming a square cross. On either side of this central motif and stretching to the edges of the bars, were similar crosses of alternating design: first four emeralds would surround a central ruby, then four rubies a central emerald, with the intervals between each design being entirely covered with great diamonds.

'The principal motif of the columns supporting the canopy was a set design in pearls, inlaid in gold.

'Of the three cushions or pillows which were upon the Emperor's throne, that behind his back was large and round like a bolster while the two others placed at his sides were flat. The cushions, and the four steps leading to the throne, were covered with precious stones.

'A jewelled sword, a damascened mace, a gem-encrusted round shield and a bow and quiver with arrows; all hung suspended from the throne.

'At length the Emperor looked up from his con-
templation and bade Baba Dost approach closer. Baba
Dost went stumblingly forward, and threw himself down
upon both knees, forehead in the dust. The Emperor
spoke:

'"O Baba Dost, the two years are complete."

'Baba Dost extended both arms at full length in abject
supplication.

'"And, my new palace?"

'Baba Dost, Contractor, emitted a strangled moan.

'"It was thy boast that it would be better than this. Pray
you well that it be so!"

'Baba Dost grovelled yet nearer the dust.

'"We desire to inspect thy handiwork!"

'The Emperor arose, and, accompanied by his eunuchs,
entered the harem by a small door to the rear of his
throne.

'He emerged presently, attired for a journey, and intimated that he would ride upon his favourite elephant. He
strode out of the palace, bidding the disconsolate Baba
Dost to accompany him.

'Eight elephants awaited the Emperor. Seven went
ahead, each bearing two men, one to guide the animal, and
the other to hold aloft the bejewelled standard attached to
a handpike.

'Immediately behind the Emperor came the Princes and
the officers of the household, all on gaily-caparisoned
horses. Also, there was the usual "small" bodyguard of
between five and six hundred horsemen, each armed with
a form of handpike to which fireworks were attached.
These rockets could propel the pikes a distance of some six
hundred yards when ignited.

'Baba Dost was mounted upon a mettlesome horse
which he had some difficulty in controlling, but under the

repeated chiding of the officers of the household he gradually forced his mount well forward in the procession until he occupied a place immediately behind the Princes. Here he was under the observation of Aziz, who looked back at him from time to time with cold, calculating eyes.

'The procession wound its way in the direction of Harim and continued its unhurried pace well into the afternoon. The Princes ahead of Baba Dost were repeating the remarks of the Emperor. Aziz, they said, would remain the night at his new palace if it pleased him, as it must, for he was assured that it was better and more magnificent than the one he had just left behind.

'The Contractor's stomach turned to water as he heard the words.

'An hour later word was passed down that the Emperor would have converse with Baba Dost. Two officers caught at the reins of his horse, and walked the animal alongside the Imperial elephant. They maintained their hold for the elephant was apt to shy at horses, and the Contractor's mount was frisky.

'"Methinks," said Aziz, "we should be seeing the minarets ere long." Dumbly Baba Dost acquiesced, for no one contradicted the Emperor.

'"The minarets are as I ordered?" Baba Dost placed both hands to his forehead in obeisance.

'"Forty spans higher than those at Damascus?" The Contractor inclined his body until his head was between his horse's ears.

'Aziz scanned the horizon. "There are not over many trees. Surely we should be seeing the walls and minarets by now?"

'"Yes, lord," gasped Baba. "Very soon now; in a few more steps; a little patience, lord – and we shall be upon the place." His eyes bulged with fear, and the sweat poured down his haggard cheeks, for he had come to his accounting and had reason to fear the worst.

'Aziz observed his perturbation, and compressed his lips into a cruel, straight line. With an impatient gesture he ordered the Contractor to fall behind, as if tired of his company.

'The procession proceeded on its way in an electric silence. The Emperor's mood had been communicated to all, and there were troubled looks, even glances of dire foreboding. None spoke to Baba Dost, and all gave him plenty of room. None would be seen in converse with him in case there was something wrong and they were suspected of complicity.

'Suddenly Aziz called a halt, and glanced around him angrily. He barked at two of his officers of state, and not too gently they bundled Baba from his horse.

'Aziz ordered the golden steps to be placed against his howdah that he might alight, and he stamped to the ground, consumed with rage.

'"This is the site," he snarled at Baba. "Where is the palace?" He pointed disdainfully at the virgin scrub, at the unplotted ground; at the utter absence of stone and mortar, let alone gold, jewels, silks.

'Inspiration came to the graceless Baba. The Emperor was a curious man. There had been occasions when sheer effrontery delighted him. Could he but nerve himself to jest, perhaps all would yet be well.

'"O, great lord," he hazarded, bowing low. "Do you not see the minarets? Observe the graceful sweep of the walls. There are the marble terraces my master ordered; there are the cascades gurgling with pure spring water . . ."

'He stopped, the better to observe the effect of his

audacious words. He saw the Emperor glance at him as if he were mad; then suddenly come to a decision.

'He advanced upon Baba, but did not strike him down with his sword. Instead he touched upon the shoulder, and complimented him upon the excellence of his art.

'"Come, my fine builder," he exhorted. "Come, and we will examine the audience chamber together."

'With a great bounding in his heart Baba took hope. Monarchs often had a sense of humour and could be excited by absurdity. He and his lord and master stalked across the barren ground.

'"See, O Essence of Kingliness," Baba expatiated, "here is the audience chamber built with the finest marble. Here, lord, is thy throne. Is it not better than that in Damascus?"

'Aziz acquiesced, smilingly. "Thou art my faithful servant," he returned, "and I am well pleased.

'"Because of thy wondrous work, thou shalt be honoured. Be my viceroy and dwell in this marvellous palace in all honour." He waved a hand to his men.

'"See," he went on, "I will even provide a bodyguard who shall see that none allows my viceroy to vacate his throne, not even for a minute."

'"Come, Baba Dost!" The Emperor's manner was ingratiating.

'He indicated the non-existent throne.

'Aziz smiled benignly. He turned to his waiting soldiers: "See," he purred, "my new viceroy upon his throne. See to it that none molests him. See also that he does not forsake his trust. Should he attempt to do so, kill him."

'He smiled into the face of Baba, then spat viciously. "Come," he ordered. "We must be gone, and on the morrow we will interview this man's bankers. A viceroy, and one under the protection of an Emperor, has no need of private riches.''

'A grunt interrupted his discourse. Baba Dost had fainted.'

5

In the Valley of Miracles

Onward again, I joined a caravan on its way to Kalat Simeon – the Castle of Simeon – rich in the early history of Syria. Daybreak found me by my camel. All was activity. As always, the life of the caravan was for me something mysterious, almost like being in a magical world.

What with shouting cameleers, hurrying pilgrims and the complaints of the caravanserai-keeper, it was a world of its own. Soon we must be off, for that elusive glimmer of a desert dawn was beginning to pale into the lustre of the risen sun, and half of the camel-riders had emerged from the serai already.

The caravan-master's rallying-drum was beating faster, and the immemorial cry of *'Rahla* – Departure!' rent the air.

The long thread of life – our caravan – was soon stretched into the distance, the sun-smitten rocks blending with the hot sand; frequently we lost our tempers, but regained them by that desert therapy, the chanting of prayers and with the expectation of arriving soon at Kalat Simeon.

Slow though our approach was to that village, I was

delighted at the sight of the many ruins that lay scattered about in the area known as Abu Barakat – the Land of Miracles.

Next morning I was informed that the caravan would stay there for nearly a week, which gave me ample opportunity to explore the region. On a plateau, some seven hundred paces long, lay the ruins: and in the heart of them was what remained of a monastery church. It was shaped somewhat like a Greek cross and some of the columns were still intact: careful examination of the various parts of the ruin revealed a remarkable correspondance with the details of the place given by Procopius.

Be that as it may, the name of Simeon is certainly fascinating – for he was a 'Pillar Hermit'. In the year 422 A.D. he mounted a pillar, and sat there in penance for no less than seven years. Later, on another column thirty-eight feet high, he spent the rest of his days. To hear his sermons from that pillar, thousands flocked to Kalat; and his pupils erected a church there in the fifth century.

The Monastery was later converted into a fort, but the sanctity of the place attracted many divines, both Christians and Muslims, and even saints who owed allegiance to no particular religion. One such was Sikandar Aga – a recluse – who gave me some details of a local cult in which he was involved .

There are, of course, countless thousands, even millions, in the East who devote themselves entirely to religion. They consecrate their minds to it; they may also consecrate their bodies. They are devotees in the highest sense of the word.

The majority of them garner from the faithful just sufficient to keep their souls within their bodies. They cannot be termed 'charlatans' even by those whom they disgust; they despise anything that savours of personal gain.

Naturally, they are not aware of the discoveries of behaviourists and other psychologists which show that even abstinence can be an indulgence.

And, in their religious fervour, they perform the most astonishing feats. One asks them why they do them and they reply, with quiet simplicity: 'This is our way to our God. You have your way. We have ours.'

I have seen, and many distinguished travellers have seen, fakirs, who, almost nonchalantly, have driven skewers through their cheeks. There was no deception about it. The skewers had just been pushed through the skin and flesh, usually one on each side of the face, and the points allowed to protrude through the mouth.

The men walked about with the skewers in position and without seeming inconvenience. Some even danced. Certainly, there was never the slightest trace of blood in any of the exhibitions which I have seen.

It is noteworthy that acupuncturists in China, and more recently in the West, have shown that needles can pierce the human body and cause anaesthesia. This is done all over the Middle East and India, both with and without assurances of a therapeutic effect. It seems a pity that no comparative studies have yet appeared in this field.

And this skewering is the least that is performed by these devotees. More than once I have seen a fakir pass a sword through his neck : not, as many may suspect, through a little of the frontal skin, but from one side to the other, just where the neck is thickest.

I am positive that there was no deception. I looked on aghast, with my teeth turning to water in acute apprehension, while the sword was being inserted, for it is no quick, impulsive motion which accomplishes the operation. It is a process which is almost too much for an observer with sensitive nerves, for it was patently obvious that considerable force was required to force the sword through the flesh. Usually, the fakir rested the hilt of the weapon upon the ground so that his entire strength could be utilized in forcing the sword through.

In one such exhibition that I witnessed, the fakir succeeded in introducing the sword so far, but no farther. The point had pierced the flesh, gone right through the neck and come against the skin on the far side of the neck. That skin must have been tough. It refused to admit the swordpoint, though the neck bulged at the spot like some monstrous bunion. It was terrifying, yet I could not avert my gaze.

Quite unconcerned, the fakir called to a colleague. With his assistance, the bulging skin was forced back upon the sword-point and the steel emerged. It continued to emerge under the ministrations of the second fakir until quite a foot of the blade was visible.

Again, there was no blood, yet I had seen a 'surgical operation' in its crudest sense.

Learned doctors may talk of the remote control of haemorrhage: with hypnosis, even in the West, 'stigmata' have been obtained in people who were very far from saints. There is, too, the matter of mental control over the processes of pain.

Continuing to develop the theme of pain, or rather its absence, let us go a step further. All this, of course, I am relating as impressions gathered when with Sikandar. One can conceivably imagine that the men who operate with skewers are novices. To force a thin rod of metal through one's cheeks may, or may not be, as fatiguing as slowly to insert a sword through the thickest part of one's neck. Certainly it would not be as dangerous and perhaps it would require less faith. But, if pain enters into these practices, and quite obviously it does not, how excruciating would be the agony to make play with the eye?

I have very vivid memories of getting an ordinary cinder in my eye. The recollection makes me wince, even as I write.

But I have seen men, worked up to a great pitch of excitement by the throbbing of drums, partially remove their eyes from their sockets, and be none the worse for it later on.

They were not abnormal. They did not have naturally protuberant eyes which might be easily removable. And, there was no trick. Indeed it seemed all too real. Perhaps though, common sense suggests, it was *I* who was hypnotised.

The men who performed this seemingly impossible operation were thought to be operating outside all knowledge and science, Western or otherwise. They were disciples of a reputed saint, and there were about a dozen of them. They danced as if maddened by the throb of drums. Each had in his hand a short metal stick, on one end of which were tiny cymbals which tinkled, bell-like, as the devotee danced.

Suddenly, at a given signal, the urging of the drums ceased. The dancers became frozen; as statues. Then, with a quick motion, they inserted the points of their metal rods under their eyelids, gave a deft twist, and their eyes had emerged from the sockets – round, amazing objects, impressing themselves upon more ordinary vision by the fact that they were thrown into dreadful relief by the eyelids which seemed to close mockingly behind them, like those of a blind man's.

Yet, these men could laugh and prance and, what is more, they could see. And, later, when they levered their eyes back into position, their sight was not in the least impaired. Neither did I at any time see the slightest suggestion of inflammation as a result of the ill-treatment which these delicate organs had received.

I have spoken only of things which I have seen and which others have seen with me. I have carefully remained within this orbit so that no one can say that I am telling *travellers' tales*.

Such displays are, of course, anathema to conventional believers. They are called tricks by mystics. But they impress all kinds of people, the gullible as well as the sophisticated.

So until a full explanation is found for them, they will continue to make a good living for those who use them to claim that they have some greater significance than they probably have.

Now certain facts about the initiation ceremony of this secret society are known: because, on payment of a staggeringly large sum, visitors can be admitted.

The novice is introduced into a room where the only illumination is from burning, aromatic tapers; drums, beaten with the hand, thud with a nerve-searing rhythm; cymbals tinkle; horns crash forth long, throaty, dolorous notes; priests chant.

The novice is presented to an altar on which is a pile of straw. The drums, the cymbals, the horns and the priests close in upon him. The rhythmic tempo of the drum quickens; the cymbals clash; the horns shriek; the priests yell into the initiate's ear.

A thick-stemmed dagger is insinuated into his hand.

'Strike, strike, strike,' thunder the priests.

The initiate, raised to a frenzy, plunges his dagger into the wheat straw again and again. Beneath the straw is glimpsed a rabbit. The initiate murders the animal with vicious stabs and those around him go berserk. They drink greedily at the blood and distribute the tiny limbs for rites even more revolting.

Through this ceremony all are within the fold. They have entered into a covenant of complicity: one of crime and necessarily, one of enforced silence.

Even the sceptic will see why there exists so little of the data which he demands.

For many of their rites, the devotees of the Black Art demand incredible prerequisites. Certainly in that unfrequented part of the world, the Syrian mountains, they profess to be able to turn themselves into wild animals and to become invisible at will.

Before they can achieve this power however, it is necessary for them to take part in protracted and evil ceremonies. Those who have come within the shadow of this sorcery must partake of a ghastly banquet.

The initiates, to the accompaniment of an extraordinary ceremonial which I am quite unable to describe, consume the bones of a newly slain goat and drink camel's milk.

The priests of this sect are hated and feared throughout the East. There, at least, there is little scepticism. Perhaps it is because the people are brought into personal contact with the powers of these fiends and, therefore, have little choice in the matter.

I have no hesitation in saying that these servants of Satan can scatter death broadcast. But how did they do it: what did their methodology add up to?

Suddenly, I realised that I held the golden key in my memory – with it, there was little difficulty in understanding the whole thing. Let us look first at the death-spell which they use.

Their usual method of causing death is through the

medium of a doll – invariably crudely fashioned in cow-dung and resembling the intended victim.

The doll is taken at dead of night to the top of a hill. There, a triangle is marked out with ashes from the funeral pyre of a goat – goats enter into many ceremonies – and within this is placed the doll.

During the incantations which follow, a variety of objects are introduced to the doll – a portion of bone from a goat, the juice from bitter lemons and, nearly always, thorns. If these are not available, the priests use needles.

The thorns (or the needles) are most important. The doll is pricked viciously with these, while the most hideous curses are invoked upon the human victim.

The theory is that it is this vicious thrusting of the thorns at the right moment which conveys the curses through the medium of the doll to the body of him or her who is presently to depart.

Always however, the victim is secretly apprised of the fate which is in store for him. Also, he is likely to discover in his path the fateful magic doll, crudely dressed in a shroud.

The golden key, of course, was something experienced by thousands of people in the West: a stage hypnosis show.

The participants in the ceremonies had been carefully hypnotised for weeks before the rituals, during their 'novitiate'.

During this time, a powerful post-hypnotic suggestion had been implanted in some that they could remove their eyes and put them back into their sockets again. Others were equally conditioned to be sure that they would actually see such a happening. *Et voilà!*

All of it was suggestion, as is the death which occurs

when someone, trained to believe it, sees the doll in his path.

I followed up another case, carried out by a community of the Salabiyya – the reputed descendants of European Crusaders, who settled in Syria. Salabiyya means 'those of the Cross, Crusaders', in Arabic.

The victim was informed that he would die. He would sicken, so he was told, as his dog sickened and when the animal died, so would he.

The dog, previously a great, healthy brute and the terror of the village, most certainly did sicken, and so did the man.

The animal's passing was painful and protracted. It was consumed with an enormous appetite and an unquenchable thirst. It became thinner and thinner. Eventually, it could not support itself on its legs and expired.

At the very moment it was said, that the dog died in the compound there was a wailing from within the house. The women of the household were mourning the death of the man who had been cursed.

I soon discovered that, although everyone believed that the two deaths had been simultaneous, they had not in fact happened at the same time. They did occur on the same day – the man after learning of the death of the dog. Further, I obtained the carcass of the dog and had some of its internal organs analysed. The report said: 'POISONED'.

It was of more than passing interest to me to hear that these folks' ancestors were said to have brought their lore from the West. Perhaps there is truth in some at least of the witch and sorcerer legends in Europe. They may even have originated there, not in the ancient East where these practices are still semi-public . . .

Having had enough of this occult atmosphere, I longed to go on with another caravan taking the desert route to Beirut. At last the chance came and I was 'wait-listed' for a caravan of pilgrims going to Mecca; I could accompany them as far as Beirut. After waiting for a full three weeks, I made ready to start on the morrow: ready, more than ready, to resume my love-affair with the caravan!

The dunes of the desert extended as far as eyes could see, like giant waves on the face of a mighty ocean, as I saw them in the early dawn from where the train of animals had rested overnight.

Now the call to morning devotions was chanted; 'Come to prayer, come to success, prayer is better than sleep!' And now we were mounting our ships of the desert for another day's journey under the grilling sun.

Many times, thirst plagued us as our line of men and camels dipped in and out of the dunes, before we arrived at last at our resting-place for that night.

Darkness was falling like an almost palpable curtain as the beasts were unloaded. Men sat round small camp-fires roasting dry camel flesh which we gulped down with hot coffee: coffee which only tastes right, somehow, when poured into tiny cups from a proper Nejdi full-beaked pot and flavoured with freshly crushed cardamoms.

We rested our weary limbs, reclining against our camel saddles in the comfort of a hip-mould scooped from the sand, and looked at the clustering stars hanging like pendant fire-jewels up above us.

The younger of two Afghan pilgrims began to relate some of the sayings and doings of a reputed Sufi of the Qadiri School of Gilan, who was well-known in Afghanistan, he said.

'Now look,' I heard myself saying, 'although Abdul-Qadir of Gilan is a famous name, there is no proof that he ever existed. Indeed, there is every reason to accept what the Sufis say about him. He was a lay-figure, designed to become a focus of tradition for historical purposes.'

The Afghans were perplexed: though, like many of their nation, they were no obsessed bigots. 'I can see that you are a man of learning,' said one, at length, after some discussion between them; 'and we would like to ask you about your opinions on some Sufic subjects.'

This placed me in something of a dilemma. My job was to visit certain dervish groups and inform them about the deterioration of their beliefs, methods and practices. So I hesitated.

'Sir,' said the elder Afghan, 'we do not know who you are, but would it help if we said that we have both been regularly admitted to the Qadiri Order?'

Technically of course, this meant that they came within my remit. I gave them some facts.

'It was not necessary for Gilani to have existed for his name to be used as a "peg" on which to hang teachings originating from the Sufis, the enlightened ones . . .'

'But,' interrupted the younger man, 'I adjure you by Allah, can this school in Afghanistan be genuine if even its leaders imagine that they are physically descended from Gilani?'

I found an opportunity to let him down lightly. 'Don't jump to the conclusion that these supposed ancients and guides are fraudulent. It is almost certain, as happens in many parts of the East, that one of their forebears followed the Qadiri discipline, and also came from Gilan, in Persia.

'Over the years and generations, the tradition becomes cloudy; the rituals become more important, the pedigree seems significant. As you well know, a person's descent is of no matter in spiritual things: so it can be simply the normal deterioration of tradition.'

One said: 'I am relieved, because we don't want to abandon our Guide, who has been a father to us, and who sent us on this journey. Perhaps he really intended us to meet up with you.'

Then the other asked me to explain why I did not wish to hear of the sayings and doings of their master.

'It's quite simple', I said, 'Sufism cannot allow ordinary records, notes, to be kept about what people say and do.'

'Why ever not? I would have thought that the most precious relics are the traditions of the teacher'.

I had to explain: 'When a teaching master is acting upon an individual or a group, whether at meetings or otherwise, all depends upon the effect which his words and actions have on the specific people present. The entire teaching-situation has been specially designed for that teacher and that learner, or those learners, alone, and for no other purpose. Indeed, it can be most harmful for the materials, the words, ideas or actions, to be used again by the participants.'

'Then,' said one of the Afghans, 'how is it that we have such voluminous records, which are known as Sufi works? Are they all superseded?'

'Not at all. But only the teaching master can tell which part of them, which words, sentences, phrases, books even, will apply to a current situation and can be useful or otherwise.'

'So it is a matter of skill?'

'No, it is a matter of knowledge.'

'Now I understand,' said the Afghan, 'why it was that the great Jalaluddin Rumi forbade his disciples to read the superb works of Attar, and spent decades writing his Masnavi. And to think that modern commentators can only assume that he was jealous of Attar . . .'

'. . . But could hardly have been, since he praised his works so lavishly,' interrupted the other.

It is quite surprising how, in large parts of the East, so little is known about its own traditions. Religious or other propaganda has often wiped out certain teachings. In other cases, the teachings have fulfilled their function, and moved on.

This situation greatly confuses the picture as far as the West is concerned. Westerners, for instance, go to the East and accept whatever people there tell them, usually in answer to questions. They seldom realise, in my experience, that Easterners will agree with you just to be polite. Or that, behind their replies, there may be axes grinding . . .

Great stars still flashed in the desert sky, a sky deep and soft like purple velvet, when we finished our hours of talk – a marathon worthy of many to which I had listened in the glens of Kabulistan.

Although another day's march lay before us, it had been well worth going without sleep, I thought; and, thinking that, I was gripped by sleep as suddenly as if by a magic spell.

The first sight I beheld on waking was the two slender minarets of a distant village mosque. That in itself was a change, because so far we had rested at night only amongst the desert sands, and risen only in the wilderness.

Soon we were in the mosque for the pre-dawn prayer. As the packed congregation around me rose and fell in the movements of divine homage, now upstanding, now bowing, now kneeling, the impression was as of trees bending in a gale in a dark forest.

The clear voice of the prayer-leader, sounding at intervals, and the whispered responses of the worshippers, seemed like the wind flowing and returning through the wooded aisles of a dense palm-grove.

Back again to the serai, and we hurried to make preparations to start on the day's journey.

The clamour, the vociferation, rose like the drone of a myriad bees: then a voice, louder than the rest – the rallying-call of the caravan leader. We were off on the lumbering camels, the tiny bells on their necks jingling merrily, and before us, once more, the desert of Allah.

That whole day, like the previous one, we crawled over the face of those sands, dragging on under the merciless sun, constant prayers arising from our straggling ranks.

At nightfall, we were at our next resting-place near a palm-grove, where, after a prayer and some food, we gathered around the camp-fire to listen to the teaching of one expert after another: a coppersmith, a jeweller, a textile merchant.

The caravan is, and must always have been, a kind of travelling university, where not only entertainment and solace were offered, but also teaching in many of the practicalities, and the theories, of life.

A poet wanted to recite a romantic ode, but one of our number, Ahmad, always cynical about love, looked up at his fellow pilgrims and said that he did not believe in such a thing; 'It is like any other pleasure; like, say possessing flowers for a time. When attained or gathered, the pleasure dies!'

We others all disagreed with him, saying that love is like a rare flower that takes root in the heart and blossoms in the soul. But the controversy had wiped the desire to recite from the poet's heart, so Ahmad won in the end.

Now the soft wind began to fan us and a new moon had

risen, looking like the silvery edge of a scimitar in the sky. We huddled down in our blankets beside our packs for the night, ready for an early start on the morrow.

The bestirring of our travelling community was like the motion of a multicoloured pageant bedecked in all the colours of the East. We were up well before dawn, because this day's march was to be a difficult one.

Now came the rallying-call, as old as history: 'Rahla, rahla!'

As the long line of our animals emerged from the palm groves, and the sun started to blaze from an empty sky over the distant crags, I knew that another blisteringly hot day was before us.

Yet in the full realization of Kismet – being in the hands of Fate – a real composure soon came upon us, as if some passing angel's hand had touched our brows in benediction. And this despite the aching backs caused, until we were thoroughly accustomed to the motion, by the lurching of our beasts.

The camels bubbled; they padded determinedly along; they spat their cud; secured to their rough backs, our litters rocked to and fro; the heat of the sun, touching the shimmering sands, rose as a distant haze, painting the bare rocks now blue, now grey, now violet.

Ever greater calmness seemed to reign around us as the vista became flatter; nothing but stretching sands extending to the very limit of one's vision.

A sense of vastness that beggars description enveloped us as we picked our way to our next resting-place along the unmarked pilgrim route, now faint, now invisible except to our guides.

Night came again, and with it ease and rest. It certainly

was a spectacular night – a night of enormous silence, of great steady pendulous stars, of gold-dusted air, as we sat gratefully after a meal around our camp fires. The Arabs, unlike many other people, seldom speak during meals. It is considered a discourtesy to the blessing of God's food.

The night was now breathing gently on us, with a touch like a soft caress: carrying a hint of the cool of the Lebanese seashore not so far to the West – our destination.

The poet spread his mat beside me to sleep. Since, he said, he hoped to have a wife some day, he agreed with my earlier words that romance was almost as great a thing as pilgrimage.

'As the saying of the Sage of the Yellow River has it,' he murmured, "Love is the gate through which every man enters the rose-garden of life".'

Another day is about to begin, a day of rejoicing, mingled for me, with regret: for it is the last one before we arrive at Beirut.

Everybody is excited, and practically everyone is already in his litter, perched on the back of a camel; the grumpy cameleers have been ready since an hour before the dawn.

But now comes the usual delay. The leader must be interrogated by half a hundred anxious folk, whose concerns are always urgent and to be resolved immediately, as he rides on a last inspection from end to end of the column. Others are praying incessantly, confident that this will add merit to their pilgrimage.

After more shouting and yelling we are about to start; when there comes a roar from the front of the train. A pack-camel has run amok, bitten the animal in front of it and kicked the one behind.

Uproar ensues. The owner of the beast is deluged with the curses of the so-recently pious ones, and it is as much as he can do to drag it by its halter out of the column.

A single rifle-shot rolls over the plain, repeating in a series of reverberating echoes. It is the caravan-leader's ultimatum, the signal for immediate departure.

That day may have been hotter than other days, but the staying-power of some of the aged patriarchs was enormous. They might have been made of hammered steel, as they rode upright on their camels or walked beside them on the burning sands.

Suddenly it seemed, the afternoon sun was declining; and we were nearing our goal – Beirut.

Beirut in the Thirties! A city in one of the most gorgeous settings to be found in this world; amidst tier upon tier of the fascinating hills of Lebanon.

Civilization had it in its grip and with a vengeance: skyscrapers, motor-cars, noise – and the smell of oil, both literal and metaphorical.

The inhabitants, other than the religious fanatics who awaited their turn, often preferred to speak French rather than Arabic. Many flocked excitedly to the casinos and the cheap and too often tawdry copies of the Western café.

Younger citizens and moneyed, vapid visitors from the Gulf, drove their cars incessantly up and down Hamra Street, impressing only each other, yet sadly, totally convinced that they were at the cutting edge of world sophistication.

I reflected that, if anyone had wanted to destroy a country and its people, they would have only to teach its young to behave like this. Surely, in due time, the place would fall apart . . .

Yet Beirut is still fighting another, and an age-long battle. Where the road emerges on the way to Damascus, there are avenues of stately pines, planted some three centuries ago by Fakhruddin, a mighty ruler of that mysterious sect, the Druse. The trees were placed there to keep the sands of the desert at bay. On this edge of the city, though, there are many sandy acres where the desert has encroached. The struggle still goes on.

Beirut made its appeal to the tourist. Its shops were filled with mementoes from the Mount of Olives in Jerusalem (made in Greece) and genuine ancient Islamic brassware and copperware (made in India).

When I was first there, the city was full of hotels, cheap ones, where you could live for almost nothing a day. In your baggage, however, there had to be a tin of insecticide and a can-opener.

There was a day of real excitement in Beirut – being present at a duel of the essentially traditional kind. A quarrel, or rather a feud, existed between two men of some standing in the neighbourhood, and a meeting had been arranged between them, which was to take place in the public market. Both, it appeared, were notable swordsmen.

The duel, surely would provide a picturesque incident. It is the kind of thing tourists always expect, when all they get is a 'Tour of the Ancient Ruins', or 'A Genuine Folkloric Evening'; ridiculous ethnicity from the Bahamas to Beijing. The triumph of hope over experience.

On the appointed afternoon, we were conducted to the part of the *souk* reserved, by local custom, for combats of the kind.

A large rectangle had been left devoid of market stalls, and was surrounded by a large and vociferous crowd.

So far there was no sign that the encounter was about to

take place, the sole source of excitement being the rather leisurely activities of a couple of boys who were doing good business selling glasses of sweet refreshing sherbet, lemon and rose flavour topped up with water, to the thirsty crowd.

At last the combatants arrived.

One was a tall, hawk-faced fellow with immense up-curling moustaches: a figure one would not care to meet on a deserted mountain pass. To my eye, he seemed to have *brigand* written all over him.

His opponent appeared younger, slimmer, but every bit as active and muscular. Indeed they seemed very evenly matched.

Drawing their swords, they advanced and – at a signal from the umpire – steel rasped upon steel.

Then a series of evolutions followed, so rapid that at times they cheated the eye. The blades locked, seemed even to coil around each other, separated, flashed, whirled.

Each man was obviously a master of his weapon, trained from boyhood to wield it so that it was at once sword and shield.

At one moment, there would be merely a snakelike silver gleam in air, the motions of which the sight could not follow. The next, there was the sword rigid as death, guarding the neck of its owner against a lightning sweep of steel.

For at least ten minutes, neither combatant appeared to have an advantage over the other and I was beginning to regard the affray more as an exhibition of skill than a serious fight. But just then, there was a dramatic development.

A thin stream of blood was now trickling down the arm of the older man. I had not seen the actual blow, for it was impossible to follow the motions of the swiftly circling blades.

The wound could not have been a very serious one, for the flow of blood was meagre, but it certainly took the attention of the crowd. They broke into a babble of sound, pointing to the crimson line on the injured man's sleeve.

The end came more suddenly than anyone had bargained for. Whether the wounded man felt his strength failing, or whether he was enraged by the shouted comments of the spectators, he appeared suddenly to grow desperate.

Whirling his weapon high above his head, he rushed upon his enemy with a raucous shout and aimed a terrible blow at him.

Like a panther, the other leapt aside so that the blow descended upon empty air. But as it came down, he thrust the blade of his own sword beneath the other's arm, so that the wrist was struck by its razor-like edge.

As the hapless swordsman was borne off, an ancient behind me spoke his mind.

'Nations and peoples who strike with the sword downward, who raise the arm thus in fight, are doomed to perish,' he intoned. 'Many times have I said so to our brother Firoz. But my counsel was not taken and now he has no sword-hand left to strike with. It is nothing less than Fate.'

It had been arranged for me to spend some weeks in Beirut, on what amounted to a crash-course in the work of the Anti-Narcotics Bureau, working in close collaboration with other countries in the area. In Turkey, many opium poppies were still grown illegally. The Druses of Lebanon and Syria protected the cannabis farmers: and both Jordan and Egypt were conduits for smugglers, mainly to the West.

I studied photographs of suspects, how to disguise myself, smugglers' hiding-places, drug chemistry and its practical uses – a remarkable curriculum, excellently put together by the Lebanese authorities.

Here, at least, there was harmony between Christian and Muslim Arabs, and even between French and English operatives.

Outside this field, the French often harboured the deepest suspicions of the perfidious British.

'They are planning to take over the world, *mon vieux*,' was the refrain.

And the British?

'Johnny Frenchman is tricky, old boy . . . All that frog-eating and wine, you know.'

During my early visits to the Levant, the Anglo-Saxon and Gallic empires were still very much alive and kicking each other.

6

The Land of Peace

The extraordinary thing about Beirut was that it was less Arabia and more 'bad imitation France' than most places one could imagine, because although the Muslim population was about fifty per cent, there was less and less Arabic spoken.

You might perhaps think that therefore, more French was spoken; and you would be wrong as I was. When first I went there by far the largest number of people spoke Italian.

Amongst the Moslems there, you would hear a good deal about the mighty Fakhruddin – a Druse prince, who with his Venetian alliance was able to achieve a form of independence in 1595; but the favours which he showed the Christians were to be his undoing.

The Lebanese show a legendary spot along the quay which is said to have suffered considerably when, in 1840, the British Fleet bombarded Beirut.

It was on my way to Baalbek – the City of the Sun-god – that I was received by Sheikh Ansari in his encampment. He persuaded me stay with him a while before going any further. To 'stay' meant going on raids with him, as I discovered too late: but fortunately, while I was there, the planned raids did not come off.

He had but recently acquired his third wife, and as she was both young and beautiful, and Ansari was also young and a merchant prince of the desert, I readily fell in with the idea of travelling with his camel-train. Our third halt was not far from Jenin; and, finding that there was an inn in the village, we resolved to stay the night there rather than make camp outside. The sun was touching the minaret tops, and men were bending low at evening prayer as our caravan wended its way up and down, and up again to the big town gates beyond which lay our destination for the night. The camels' hairy necks were shaking their tiny jingling bells as the camel-train passed a shrine, as we were entering the place.

'Peace and prosperity,' shouted a townsman from under his thatched roof to Ansari, Sheikh of the desert, my companion and host: 'Carry ye the silk and amber of Egypt to the markets of the city of minarets and domes?'

The leader of the caravan, though proud and young and haughty, returned the salutations of this peasant. Then he counted his rosary beads, as I reminded him not to speak to a stranger – a stranger outside the city gates. For I had remembered the recent words of a holy man whom we had met: 'Speak not, O Wayfarer,' the saint had told us, 'to any stranger beyond the city gates, unless thou wish'st thy most cherished thing to vanish.'

It was disregarding that advice which was to cost Ansari dear . . .

Sheikh Ansari turned in his saddle to see whether all was well with his lumbering camels. As he did this, fear stole into his heart – a fear not for the rich merchandise he carried or the spices of Ind that he could buy and take back to Arabia's distant shores. He feared for the steed he

102

mounted, the horse that he had reared and fed on milk –
and milk is scarce, and dearer perhaps than the blood of
men, in that desert and dessicated hilly land.

Ansari had waited and watched and tended this one
great treasure of his heart, this matchless white steed of
Arabia, with which he would have refused to part for twice
the ten thousand palace domes of Samarkand.

In that gloaming that divides, like a thin strand of
golden ribbon, night from day, tinkled and tinkled the
bells on the necks of his hundred camels, as our caravan
jostled and jangled its way between the yawning gates of
the Caliph's city – the Caliph that was. Like a black streak
the caravan, so richly laden, moved on over the pale face of
the burning sands.

Boys, men, old and young, welcomed Sheikh Ansari to
the inn. The innkeeper had roasted a whole desert gazelle
in his honour. For you should know that Ansari was both
rich and popular, and he parted with his gold as readily as
sinners part with their virtues.

The prayer-caller had called us all to prayer and now, all
our muleteers and camelboys were busy lighting their
fires, like so many glow-worms in that vast inn; the
bearded Sheikh reclining against a camel-saddle told his
beads in silence. There was much for which the Sheikh of
the desert had to thank Allah, I thought. A thousand
pieces of gold and more he would receive for his merchandise; and then I saw my host's eyes alight upon that
tethered form of beauty, on his horseflesh beyond
compare.

A thing which he would not barter for the twin rivers of
Babylonia that watered his land and gave dates to the
world. Men styled his horse *Son of the Mother of Stars* –
Son of the Milky Way.

These thoughts, I realised, must have been in Ansari's

mind, as I saw him doze off, but hardly had he been asleep ten minutes when: 'Ya Ansari!' – the shout rang out in the inn.

As is the custom with the desert warriors, the Sheikh's hand instinctively sought his scimitar, for rudely awakened men think not instantly of the difference between friend and foe.

And then, out of the darkness, loomed the caller, none other than Ansari's best friend and compatriot, another mighty warrior and clan-leader, Sheikh Akram.

'Peace and prosperity be upon thee, O Ansari!' said Akram. 'My hair has grown grey in thinking of thee. Thou hast tarried long in thy oases, and methinks that thy train grows larger, Allah be praised!

'And tell me, brother Ansari, of thy welfare, of the health of thy children. Ah! and tell me, too, Ansari, of the desire of my heart, of the Son of the Milky Way – that peerless horse.'

Ansari acknowledged the salutation of his old friend. 'Come and sit ye down, brother. But what is it that weighs in thy hand?'

''Tis but a bag of gold pieces, the price of something I would buy,' I heard Akram say.

As sons of two powerful neighbouring chiefs, they had learned the arts of war and peace together. They were of an age, and each had loved and lost together, for each of their respective wives had died young. The spell that a woman casts upon the men of the warrior clans is one which knows no severance, not even that of death.

In blood feuds and forays, Akram and Ansari had ridden to victory: if Ansari had grown rich by trading, Akram was not less wealthy. Though his palm groves had been cut down to the roots, from the ground gushed forth 'the fat of the earth' which is what they call oil and which some

Western companies shared with him, to their mutual benefit.

Ansari, therefore, was truly happy to greet his old friend – but he loved one thing more than Akram; he loved his noble Arab horse.

'For once, my brother, thou and I find our minds not in agreement,' said my host to Akram. 'The desire of thy heart, this prince of the desert which I have reared, seems to be thy craving also. Dost thou not see him just there, tethered, whipping the gloom with his moonlit tail? And I, O Akram! I shall not part with him till the crack of doom!'

Akram gulped the third cup of coffee which denoted dismissal, and gave a hearty laugh as he rose to grasp his friend's hands in bidding him goodbye.

'My heart is set upon thy horse, O my friend,' he said, 'and maybe the crack of doom will be tonight, for though I may not fight with thee, I might buy or steal thy horse.

'A thousand gold pieces I would gladly give you as the price of the Son of the Milky Way.'

At this, Ansari became wrath and although the ebony of the dark night hid the colour that mounted upon his cheeks, he only whispered hoarsely in suppressed anger:

'Speak not thuswise, O Akram! Speak not again of it! Speak no more of the Son of the Milky Way, and begone! Begone, before my scimitar bares its face, and stares at thine!'

But there was one thing about Akram: when he set his mind upon a thing, he usually got it.

Ansari, anxious in mind, rose from his seat and secured his horse firmly to the camel's saddle before bowing in the recital of his last prayer of the evening.

'Akram, I swear by the Name of Allah, is a great one, a mighty swordsman and a mightier thief! But, by the beard of the Holy Sage, I am a mightier thief-catcher.'

He gasped in amazement when, his prayer over, I handed him a bag of gold pieces. It had been left where Akram sat: a bag of coins ... and Ansari became distraught.

This meant, he thought, the severance of generations of friendship between their two houses, for if those gold pieces meant the price of the horse of which Akram had spoken, 'Then by God!' said the Sheikh to me, 'I, Ansari, the son of Ansari, shall slay Akram this night.'

He had spoken too soon however, for a shape immediately descended upon my merchant Sheikh; his own scimitar struck only the wooden pommel of the camel's saddle, and we were both soon gagged and bound at gunpoint.

Anon we heard, in some agitation, the Son of the Milky Way being galloped off; huddled and helpless, Sheikh Ansari and I, with the bag of gold between us, tried to peer through the darkness of the gate to the inn. We could just make out, fleetingly, the rump of the horse being swallowed in the gloom of the desert night.

It is the custom amongst the gallant men of Arabia to accept such events by invoking their inborn sense of humour, and Ansari next morning said but little, as he led his train out of the inn. Leaving the bag of a thousand golden pieces with the inn-keeper, to him he said:

'If you see Akram, give him this gold. Gold I do not seek.' And the rest of the story I heard from the Sheikh himself on my next meeting with him.

Weeks and months passed it seemed, and the yearning for his horse remained in Ansari's heart. Although he sold much and bought even more from the souks, thus growing richer and richer, his mind was not at peace.

All he really wanted now from life was the horse, that one and no other. Yet, searched he high and low amongst the groves or the crowded bazaars, or sent he word to

Akram in his desert fastness, an oblivion seemed to have swallowed all trace of Akram and the Son of the Milky Way.

When many moons had passed, and Ansari still found his wound deepening, he resolved to go to Damascus or even to the lair of Akram himself to seek the Son of the Milky Way. He would regain the animal, at all costs.

And it was on the very day when he set foot in that city of domes and minarets that he heard from the inn-keeper that Akram had refused to take back the gold. And that, that very day he was expected to come to the city for the Friday prayer.

That was enough for Ansari and, donning a beggar's garb, he shuffled his way out of the city gates.

It was still some hours before the midday prayer, and from yonder towering hills, through those cedar groves, down the path beside the Shrine of the Holy Priest, lay the route that Akram must take, and there in the shade of a cluster of dusty date palms did Ansari sit, waiting and watching.

The countryfolk from all around, leading their beasts of burden, were now trekking towards the gateway. They came in twos and threes, singly, in groups, on prancing desert mares, limping donkeys, or merely following their womenfolk on foot, all treading in their several ways, chanting, singing, or telling their rosary beads on that holy day of the week. From each and from all did Ansari seek alms.

'Give, in the Name of Allah. Give on the Holy Day,' he intoned as they passed. And many a silver and copper coin tinkled into the beggar's bowl. Ansari waited patiently, his eyes glued to the bend of the road on yonder incline.

Then he saw it. As if a streak of sheer whiteness had leapt the side of the hill. With it, too, did his heart leap, for it was none other than Akram who came: mounted on the desire of his heart.

'Give, my Lord, in the Name of Allah,' cried Ansari, as Akram came near.

The rider pulled in his horse.

'Wilt thou not, Lord, now give a poor beggar a ride upon thy beauteous horse; as far as the mosque, where beggars and kings may pray together on this holy day?' said Ansari to Akram in an assumed tone. 'For see ye not, Noble One,' and the beggar pointed to his bare feet swathed in old rags, 'that I can walk no further than the miserable shade of these sparse trees?'

An Arab, the saying goes, more often than not is schooled in the chivalry of ten thousand generations. Akram was one such. Proud, yet generous, he dismounted and helped the beggar into the saddle.

'Thus, indeed,' he said to Ansari, 'thou shalt ride this day, even as the king himself rides to the prayer! And know thou, O beggar, that thou sittest upon the finest horseflesh ever born or bred in this vast desert.

'And I, I a Sheikh, will walk beside thee on my own good feet. For thus I might win some acceptance in the eyes of the Most Generous One Who neither sleeps nor eats, but lives for ever.'

The disguised man realised that the horse had sensed that his true owner was on its back. It was ready to fly. In a trice Ansari had dug his heels into the flanks of his horse.

Like lightning it jumped. Ansari now threw off his beggar's cloak, and galloped far into the desert: but soon he came back and he said to Akram:

'Take my horse, O Akram, and also thy thousand pieces of gold, lest word goes round the desert that thou lost thy mount through giving help to a beggar; for thus charity could vanish from our people.' And so the desert code of honour was kept intact.

Thence to the city of the Sun-God, ancient Baalbek. The Sheikh had provided me with an escort as there was a blood-feud amongst the tribes.

The great Temple of Jupiter has gone, but the Temple of Bacchus was a dream, though a broken dream – this Baalbek.

Standing upon its own stylobates, the enormous columns still loom around it. At the entrance, the beautiful tracings of leaf and fruit, celebrating the glorious vine, are there for all to see.

And the gigantic blocks of stone in the walls of the temple! Blocks, sixty-four feet in length, ten feet thick and twenty-five in height. How were they transported over the mountains? How were they put in place?

Six enormous columns are all that remain of the glorious Temple of Jupiter – six silent symbols of a mighty past.

Sitting astride one of the columns, I espied an Arab in typical flowing garb. He rose to meet me as I advanced. He wore patent leather shoes. And how pointed! I asked him where he got them.

He said: 'I am not surprised that you covet them; but know, I would not part with them for a king's ransom!

'There is probably not another pair like this on the face of the earth. You may well have to go as far as the Land of the Jinns, the genies, to find their like.

'Stranger, abandon your unhealthy, greedy desire for my unique shoes, and may the Evil Eye of covetousness be far!'

I apologised, and withdrew, invoking the Name of Allah to counteract any malevolence I might have let loose.

As I wanted to see Christmas festivities at Jerusalem, I hurried back from Baalbek southwards to Damascus, and thence by devious ways to a point to the north of the Holy City.

Farther south – Jerusalem, and not the Jerusalem seen by so many flying tourists, but *Al Quds*, The Holy, to the Arabs – in Muslim tradition the second city to Mecca in sanctity and of which the Holy Koran itself speaks.

Few Christians, whose knowledge of their faith has been drawn from such sources as Sunday School and church services, are aware of the close relationship between their own religion and that of the Muslims.

Yet it is in Jerusalem that the two faiths meet.

Towering and barren cliffs rose right and left of me as I approached Jerusalem from the north-west; the sensations in my mind were of an anticipation of awe, almost a blending of a discoverer's enthusiasm with a pilgrim's devotion.

A high rugged pass it was through which my pony carried me, but presently the terrain changed. Stunted bushes gave place to dwarf olive trees, more trees followed, then a grove; now men and women spread their white sheets under the shade of the trees, heaping the purple, oily fruit upon them.

A little further under these trees sat a shepherd, his flock wandering nearby, their black tails moving as the lambs darted in between the twisted trunks of the olive trees. A stream trickled sedately.

Now the man climbed up the terrace, his flock following. He held a lamb in his arms, his robe swaying a little, a long hooked stick in hand. Reaching the stream, he carefully washed the lamb in it.

The stillness of the scene, the peacefulness of that picture, engraved itself on my mind. Had Jesus, too, not walked that way? Yes, the drama of ages was virtually there for the seeing.

The day being Christmas Eve, Jerusalem was packed with sightseers: pilgrims one could hardly call them, with their cameras, large horn-rimmed spectacles and big tips to the religious guides.

It was just past the hour of my morning prayer, when I hurried to the Church of the Holy Sepulchre, trying to be the first to view the many ceremonies that take place there.

Some hopes! I could hardly get into the courtyard of the Church, let alone the interior. Hundreds had slept outside the Holy Precincts the night before to gain early admittance.

How was I to get in? Naively, I had not imagined that there would be a difficulty. Now it seemed impossible.

Then I remembered a high dignitary of one of the Christian denominations who was, in fact, a Sufi. Naturally, this fact was not widely known.

People in the West thought of such people as 'Mohammedan monks' at best, and 'charlatans' at worst. Indeed, in the East, the teeming masses of alleged Sufis, really imitation dervishes or adventurers, were one of the causes of the downfall of the Turkish Empire and the anti-religious activity of the great Mustafa Kemal. Europe too, had had its own phase of fraudulent priests and vitiated monks, particularly in the Middle Ages.

But my Archbishop was glad to help – and soon I was smuggled in by a private door.

Whilst I waited for influence to get me into the Church, the crowd had increased. Arabs, Armenians, Copts and people of many European countries closed in on the gate.

Reverently they stood, muttering prayers, crossing and recrossing themselves, rubbing holy oil into their hair, buying trinkets, glass beads or olive wood crosses made by the Christian Arabs of Hebron, to be prized ever afterwards as sacred relics.

Inside the Church at last, the simplicity of the place overpowered me. A dim, religious light shone through the window, while on one of the balconies, a choir sang and filled the space with moving music.

Here and there, women bent low before altars on uncovered stone floors; a priest was blessing the rosaries of some Arab youths near a slab where the body of Christ is believed to have been anointed.

People were crossing themselves from right to left three times and then kissing this stone as they entered.

Up above, the enormous dome was supported by square pillars; the walls around were mildewed and, architecturally, it did not compare favourably with Italian churches. But what is stone and mortar in such matters?

The object of greatest sanctity, the Sepulchre itself, stands in the centre of the rotunda. It is, in fact, a domed shrine about twenty-five feet in height. Some sixteen columns surround it, but the twisted stones of those ornamented columns, where its door is, have a beauty all their own.

Passing under an arched door, I stood before the raised marble edifice, very like an Eastern grave. It was not much more than six feet long.

A Greek monk, tall, grim and stately, stood reciting prayers; he held a peasant boy by the arm, blessing him all the while as the youth bent his knees before the mighty tomb.

A rosary had fallen from the hand of an old woman as, overcome with religious fervour, she emerged from the little room; tears streamed, riding over her wrinkled face.

Nearby, a group of Copts were singing lustily, their hymns in Arabic; the long tassels of their red tarbushes moving to and fro over their sallow faces.

Having lit small tapers, men and women were disappearing into vaults to have described to them the various places said to be connected with their Saviour.

Outside once more, the crowd had melted away but small boys still ran hither and thither selling holy glass rosaries and olive-wood crosses; the worshippers were coming in and out, procession after procession.

Priests in black cloaks, choir boys in white robes, the Patriarch in dazzling raiments of scarlet and gold. A choir singing, then another chanting; and over it all the great bells clanged and chimed.

And there arose from a thousand throats, a medley of hymns that would surely have moved even the greatest of all pagans with their emotion.

Unlike any other town, Jerusalem does not seem to suffer ups and downs in its ordinary life caused by the occurrence of such ceremonies at Christmas and Easter, for the devout atmosphere is always present – it is part of the everyday.

Perhaps that is why a considerable number of worshippers follow the Franciscan fathers on their procession every Friday along the Via Dolorosa.

If you have even the slightest religious feeling, seeing these venerable men take the Way of Sorrow on which Jesus walked bearing the Cross will bring home the fact that, this materialistic age notwithstanding, men can yet suffer eagerly for their conviction: only a short way from immorality and the hilarity of vice and wine.

There are fourteen stations where white-bearded monks, wearing sandals, sun-helmets, and thick blanket coats, kneel and recite prayers on this Way of Agony in the grilling heat of the midday sun. The procession is led by Muslim mace-bearers, through bazaars, up and around the cobbled streets of Jerusalem.

Later, see also how a Christian Arab salutes his Muslim fellow-countrymen, how they greet each other – 'Good Morning' – they shout to one another with a smile, and feel the love of good neighbourliness. Here more than in any other part of the world, they appreciate that both are 'People of the Book'.

A Muslim's heart, however, goes out to the Holy Place which encompasses the Aqsa, the 'Farthest Mosque' mentioned in the Koran itself, and to the Rock which was the scene of the Prophet's night-journey to the Celestial Throne.

On entering the gigantic quadrangle, you see an edifice surmounted by a golden dome about seventy feet high. This is the Dome of the Rock. Standing on a raised platform, it dominates the landscape.

Discarding my shoes as I went in, I beheld a thing, the like of which my eyes had never seen.

Light fell upon a gigantic grey-red rock below, on a stone with ripples and twists in undulations. All in a piece, some sixty feet long, it lay there like something living.

The hoofprints in the rock left by Buraq, the Prophet's steed, were pointed out. I prayed in a crypt under the rock, reached by descending eleven steps. It is surrounded by a railing almost my own height, and I am a tall man.

The effect of the light entering the interior through the coloured glass windows was marvellous. The ceiling is painted with dull gold; the floor is of marble mosaic. The richness of decoration inside brings home to the worshipper how little sacred things need man's hand to beautify them.

There are many arches on the platform on which the Dome stands, and then the worshipper descends to pray in the Mosque, second only to Mecca in sanctity. Sycamore trees frame it and its marble arches, bathed in glowing sunshine.

Not dissimilar to the great Omayyad Mosque, at Damascus, it is a beautiful building. For its reconstruction and repair in the nineteen-thirties, the then Grand Mufti of Jerusalem was chiefly responsible.

Here, as in other Muslim buildings, the Nizam of Hyderabad's name is shown as a donor of the help which was needed for its repair: nobly has the native carver's hand effected the ravishing beauty of its inner domes and carved niches.

Curious to relate, both Christian and Muslim festivals seem often to occur on Fridays. One might be in the morning, the other in the afternoon, or even concurrently, but never is there a communal or religious riot or unpleasantness on that score.

One Friday while I was there, a Christian procession was passing up the Via Dolorosa; while most of the Arabs were crowding into the adjoining streets to celebrate an occasion at the Tomb of Moses.

Muslim Arabs trek from all corners of the northern desert to Jerusalem for this Feast of Nabi Musa (the Prophet Moses) and a three days' gala fair is held at the reputed tomb of the Lawgiver.

From early morning on that Friday, there were little streams of peasant Arabs trickling down the brown-grey valleys in the environs of the Holy City.

Bedecked in their brightest clothes, new cloaks, embroidered headgear – some using staffs painted in many
colours, they were on their festive march to Jerusalem.
Women came too; their long skirts trailing behind them.
A little before the Friday midday prayer, the Temple
Mount was full of celebrants; and as soon as the prayer was
over, their procession started for the tomb of Moses.

I watched them as they went, dancing a hopping sword-
dance, slashing the empty air with shining blades, and
singing the praises of Moses. Green and black banners
were carried behind the mount of a Sayed, a prince, the
leader of their procession.

Women came with their male relatives and enjoyed the
yearly open-air bazaars of Nabi Musa; but only until dusk.
After that, they had to cook the 'sacred cakes' to be
distributed amongst the poor. 'Thuswise,' says the Arab
tradition, 'the great Nabi is pleased to recommend a good
season of olives.'

In the Eastern Mediterranean, this eating of sacramental bread is an age-old custom, not confined to Christianity and much pre-dating it.

And so, in singing and feasting, in buying and selling,
the three days of rejoicing for Nabi Musa were happily
spent.

A visit to the Holy Land reminds one how difficult it is
to understand Christianity without reference to its Eastern, and Semitic, roots. The Greek, Roman and later
Western European filters through which the ideas and
images have passed, have clearly produced a distortion in
its modern presentation.

Friends here gave me some background information on
the Inn at Bethlehem where the historical Church of the
Nativity, marking the birthplace of Jesus, is situated.

On my first visit there, in the early nineteen-thirties, it had just become the subject of intense archaeological discussion.

While repairs to the building were being carried out, mosaic flooring was found some three feet below the existing level of the church. An unexpected find like this in such a sacred shrine naturally awakens more than ordinary interest.

It was Constantine, the first Christian Emperor, who had erected a basilica at Bethlehem over a cave which was, at that time, believed to mark the spot of the Nativity.

That was in the year AD 330. Some two centuries later, Justinian carried out certain repairs to the structure. From that day to this, the historic building was only supposed to have received ordinary attention in the matter of renovations and repairs, and it was generally believed that the main features of the Basilica stood as Constantine had erected it.

The discovery of the mosaic floor raised two interesting questions: to what period in history does the present building belong; and, more interesting still to the lay mind, what effect does the discovery have upon the claim that this was the site of the birthplace of Jesus?

Before attempting to answer these questions let us first note how the discovery came to be made and also the reason that led Constantine to accept this spot as the site of the Nativity.

One William Harvey, a noted architect, was brought out to Jerusalem by the Government of Palestine, to advise what should be done to preserve the Church of the Holy Sepulchre.

Mr. Harvey was officially connected with the British Office of Works, his business being the preservation of ancient buildings and monuments. He was an expert in this type of work, particularly with regard to large domed buildings. The walls of the Church of the Holy Sepulchre were at that time bulging to a dangerous degree, caused by the weight of the dome.

While in Jerusalem, he was asked to inspect the Church of the Nativity at Bethlehem. He recommended certain necessary repairs, particularly the strengthening of the pillars bearing the roof. While excavating near one of the pillars in the church a section of a mosaic floor was revealed. This was an unexpected find and newspapers started to ask: 'Was Jesus really born in a rich household?'

The opening was enlarged and it was seen that the mosaics covered a wide area. The whole floor of the Church was then taken up and it was found that three feet or so below its present level lay a beautiful mosaic pavement. Did this mark the floor of the original Church and, if so, why was it covered up in this way?

The mosaics are of exceptionally fine quality, the design being in the form of a floral scroll, a pattern which was in vogue in Byzantine times. There is an entire absence of the animal and human figures so characteristic of the mosaic work of the fifth and sixth centuries.

Again, the four rows of columns that support the roof of the side aisles and the upper walls of the nave were built in connection with a floor the level of which must have been approximately the same as that of the present floor.

This conclusion is confirmed by the fact that the mosaic pavement ends in a broken edge running parallel to the sides of the foundation walls supporting the colonnades.

Further excavations have shown that this mosaic pavement not only covered the present nave of the Church, but extended also into the apse.

The present apse is triapsidal in plan, but the mosaic

flooring here indicates that originally, the apse was octagonal in design. The flooring of this octagonal apse is divided into two sections, between which there is a raised circular structure, through which a small hole permits a view of a sacred grotto below. Not only does this aperture permit a sight of the grotto, but through it a beam of light penetrates into the cave.

Since nothing had been found indicating a structure earlier than this mosaic pavement, the conclusion which Mr. Harvey and other experts reached was that the mosaics mark the floor of the original Church which Constantine erected on this site. How much more of his work survives incorporated into the structure of the present building it is impossible to say.

It is evident, however, that the Basilica he erected had a central nave and four side aisles, and that the width of the Church was identical with that of the present structure.

The apsidal transepts, however, which form the most striking feature of the present building, did not exist in the original plan, Constantine favouring an octagonally-shaped apse. Indeed, Constantine's church must have been almost totally demolished before the present Basilica could be erected.

But the question which mostly concerns the lay mind is not so much whether the present Church dates back to Constantine's day, but whether the discovery throws any fresh light upon the authenticity of the grotto as the birthplace of Jesus.

As far back as AD 100, Justin Martyr repeats a tradition current in his time that a certain cave in Bethlehem had been sanctified by the birth of Christ.

Then, early in the second century, the Roman Emperor Hadrian is said to have destroyed a church which stood on Christ's birthplace at Bethlehem and erected in its place a temple to Adonis. In laying some new flagstones in the courtyard of the Church, a vaulted subterranean chamber was found by modern archaeologists, and thought to be the remains of Hadrian's pagan temple.

This all tends to indicate that the present Church stands over the cave which the Christians of the first century believed to be the place of the Nativity. This underground chamber, which has been accepted for so long as the birthplace, lies below the Greek or main portion of the Church, and is reached by a circular staircase. It is forty feet long, twelve feet wide and ten feet high. The walls are lined with marble, and the floor is paved with the same material.

At the bottom of the steps is an altar beneath which, set into a marble slab, is a silver star, which is claimed to be the exact spot of the Nativity and hallowed accordingly. Opposite this altar are three steps leading down to another altar, where stood the manger in which the Virgin Mother is said to have laid her child.

Here it is interesting to note what the writers of the New Testament have to say in regard to the matter of the manger. After all, that is the best authority available.

Significantly, in the two Gospel narratives – St. Matthew and St. Luke – which deal with the birth of Jesus, no mention is made of a cave, stable, barn, or anything equivalent.

Matthew, speaking of the Wise Men, even says: 'And when they were come into the *house* they saw the young child with Mary, his Mother.' (Matt. ii. 11). There is no mention here of a stable, only a house.

True, Luke, in recording the event, refers to a manger. He tells us how the shepherds 'found Mary and Joseph and the babe lying in a manger.' (Luke ii. 16).

But, if you consider the local conditions, what Luke

meant is pretty evidently not the manger of a recognized stable, but the manger found in an ordinary home of the place and time.

The interior of peasants' dwellings in Palestine are divided into two sections, one being the living quarters of the family, while the other serves as a shelter for cattle.

The family occupy an upper platform, known as the *mastaba*; the cattle are accommodated below and this stable portion of the dwelling is known as the *ruya* – the area of the watering-trough; a sort of natural bassinet.

When visitors come, and there is no room for them on the *mastaba*, they sleep and live in the *ruya*. The cattle are turned out; mats and rugs are laid on the floor and all is made as comfortable as possible.

No cattle occupy the *ruya* while it is used for guest accomodation. Indeed, I have frequently passed such dwellings at night and noticed animals tied to rings in the wall outside, an indication that the *ruyas* were at that time being used by relatives or friends of the owner.

In nearly all *ruyas*, there is a small raised place, a crude manger, on which the owner may sleep at night. This enables him to keep a watch over the newly-born lambs, lest in the crowded quarters some get crushed or trodden on by larger animals.

Here too, he often sleeps for preference on a cold night, for the animals help to keep him warm. Should a baby be born in a *ruya*, this manger-ledge would naturally be found a handy and safe place in which to lay it.

We are all acquainted with pictures and Christmas cards depicting the Infant Jesus surrounded by cattle. If you show such a picture to the peasants of Palestine, however, they will look at you with surprise and declare that, in that country, no child is ever actually born in the presence of cattle or allowed to remain among them.

Whether the caverns below the Church at Bethlehem were once above ground and formed the *ruyas* or basements of private houses one cannot say.

It is the opinion of the writer that they represent rather the conventional stable portion of the inn where Joseph and Mary sought shelter. The caverns are situated close to the market-place at the junction of the main roads into the town: the very place one would expect to find a village inn.

Furthermore, the stabling at these Eastern inns is often nothing more than a crude shelter, partially excavated out of the rocky ground and often partly subterranean.

If we accept the Church of the Nativity as marking the site of the inn where Joseph and Mary sought shelter, and the peasants' belief that Christ was born in the *ruya* of a private house, which took in guests, it is in keeping with the gospel narrative.

The Church at Bethlehem is still of great historic interest, for it is likely that it was here that Joseph and Mary found accommodation that night. Those Christmas mangers, however, are another matter . . .

Before I left Jerusalem, the eminent theologian who was my host introduced me to one of the least-expected experiences of my life. He demonstrated how to use a Magic Box.

According to both the Jewish and Arabian cabbalistical traditions, letters, words and numbers are charged with power.

Magical boxes are made of metal, usually three metals – brass, silver and copper – and generally engraved with numbers or words.

These engravings may betoken the alleged power of the box to grant wishes, or may be general in application. The lore of the magical box seems, nowadays, to be known to a very few; formerly, I was told, they were better known; but now . . .

Some of the boxes are like tiny chests; others, like pouches, are worn at the waist.

Their use is quite simple. The problem is to find one. Whatever the person wishes to bring about is written on a piece of virgin (previously unused) paper.

This paper is put into the box and left for the *Jinn* presiding over it to accomplish. Some take quite a time to act: others can be instantaneous, my informant assured me.

There is one other requirement. As with other metal objects collected by magicians (like Aladdin's lamp): the box or other object (sometimes they are trays, sometimes metal pendants) has to be 'charged' with *Baraka*, by 'blessing' it with magical or higher power.

People who can perceive this quality may collect such objects. Sufis are supposed to be pre-eminent in this Recognition of Blessing.

In the shops, on a tour with my friend the magician-priest, I was shown some items on sale which were supposed to have the Baraka, and other objects which were said to be quite devoid of it.

Alas, I lacked the quality or perception myself to tell the ordinary from the magically-charged.

The Lost City of The Desert

The low-roofed stone houses perched on the rocky terraces of the valley reminded me of Simla, the Indian
mountain station, and formerly the summer capital of the
British Raj – only without the lush Himalayan vegetation.
But this was Jordan: then Transjordan, not a kingdom
yet, but merely an Emirate with a new palace for the Emir.
Its sprawling, little capital lay eastwards from Jerusalem
beyond the Allenby Bridge.

Heels clicked and the guard presented arms as the car
pulled up in front of the palace. It was, I thought, a great
honour for a mere wanderer like me to be saluted in this
manner. But extraordinary courtesy is the hallmark of the
Hashemites, whether monarchs or otherwise.

Soon I saw a fairly short, quite thick-set man standing
under a flood of lights in the entrance.

Emir Abdullah himself had come out to meet me. This
truly was the old-world Arabian courtesy of his forebears
– Abdullah traced his ancestry back directly to the
Prophet.

The first impression of this third son of Mecca's Sharif

Husein was of a benevolent-looking scholar – a man who has just emerged from a brown study.

The impression persisted during dinner; for at his table there sat Arabs, Turks, Syrians, Persians and even Europeans: the food, too, was international in character.

The latter point is of importance, since practically every item on the table, not excepting even salt, was imported from the adjoining countries; for Transjordan's resources were but meagre in this regard.

He spoke neither like a monarch, nor yet as a diplomat. There was no stiff-neckedness about him: he did not choose his words with any ponderous deliberation, but spoke and laughed like a normal, warm but courtly human being. Yet his knowledge of affairs and men was extremely comprehensive.

He even knew more about the Indian and Javanese Muslims, among whom I had spent time, than most Arabs. He talked about the Afghan King Amanullah, whom I had interviewed, and his notorious top hat. He was as insistent about the need for progress in propaganda and education as any Western publicist.

Emir Abdullah begged me to ask the Afghan savant and Sufi sage, Sirdar Ikbal Ali Shah, (also a direct and highly-honoured descendant of the Prophet) to visit him again; which I am happy to say he subsequently did.

The Emir said he wanted elucidation from his Hashemite kinsman of some of the knottier problems in understanding the master-works of Rumi.

He and his father had always studied them with much affection, and in the original classical Persian at that: which he read and spoke well.

Years later, I was delighted to be able to fulfil several private and delicate commissions for this courtly gentleman: the salt of the earth. He, never forgetful, sent me an extraordinarily generous present.

The Hashemites have a reputation in the East of giving to others in accordance with their own importance: not that of the recipient!

Of a grand Arab Federation, he spoke with more than ordinary conviction and hope.

'But, My Lord!' said a green-turbaned courtier newly returned from the pilgrimage to Mecca, far to the south; taken over from the Hashemites after the First World War: 'Would these Wahhabeen, Bin Saud's fanatics now installed in Arabia, allow . . .'

The Emir cut the man short. 'Sir, I guess your meaning,' he said, 'And I also know the sad result of the Wahhabi raids upon your village.' He counselled the man in detail, anticipating in great detail the future course of events in Desert Arabia.

Then the Emir Abdullah bade me take a message to the Muslim world.

As a non-Arab, I had been collecting declarations from Islamic leaders. British (and other colonial powers') Intelligence Services effectively blocked their lines of communication – in those days at least.

No colonial or protectorate subject or citizen could get a passport without extensive political checks. Even then, the arrivals and departure of such innocents were also logged by British, French and other agents at ports and points of entry and exit to other countries.

The system was extremely efficient. It covered most of what is now the Third World, with but few exceptions: the chief of these, at the time, being Ethiopia, Iran and Afghanistan. The Old World was effectively divided up between Britain, France, Italy, Spain, Portugal, The Netherlands and even Belgium.

As I told the Emir, the Sirdar Shah's introduction had gained me audiences with the Shah of Persia and the Turkish President, as well as with the Emir himself.

'As the Ghazi of Turkey, and the Shah Pahlavi of Iran have given messages!' he now addressed me, 'I, too, will send a word to my co-religionists.

'The hearts of my own family, as well as yours, know what the Wahhabis have done to us. But, be you all who are present here, my witnesses, that I say it in all honesty that I bear [the Saudi King] Bin Saud no ill-will. He guards Allah's House, in Mecca, and may Allah help him, and give us strength to assist him too.

'Our past quarrels are like writing on the sand. They are gone, the Arab nation is one, to be led by the servants of Al Islam.'

The Emir spoke with such earnestness that it is impossible to forget the scene. We listened in intense silence; a man who had been a Wahhabi fundamentalist rose as one possessed, and kissed the hands of that truly great Arab Prince.

In spite of the restrictions imposed by the European nations, it was still possible to travel around the Islamic world to some extent, providing that one made extensive plans. I was in Amman partly to speak to a group of a dozen clerics from the especially secret Nusairi Sect.

They had travelled here, quite exceptionally, from some of their chief countries of residence: Iraq, Syria, Lebanon, Palestine.

They are said to be so secretive that none has ever revealed the secrets of their books, their beliefs or their rituals. It had been thought that they are a remnant of the ancient star-worshippers of the Levant, the Mandeans, and that they believe in reincarnation. For most people, that is the sum total known about them.

The Sufis had decided to give the Nusairis some information, instead of the other way about, and they had jumped at the opportunity.

Their High Priest was fascinated to hear me say that, according to the Sufis, human knowledge in the religious field was divided into three ranges:

1 *Exoteric* (*Zahiri*)
2 *Intermediate* (*Wasiti*)
3 *Esoteric* (*Batini*)

'But this is exactly what we ourselves hold!' he exclaimed. 'The only difficulty is that we do not know how to pass from one stage to the next. Please elucidate, if you are permitted by your oath'.

I told him that I would gladly do so, and that no oath bound me in this respect. I was limited only by what I did and did not know.

'This,' he told his companions, 'may well be what we mean by the tradition coming back from the Spring, the Well, of the East.'

This, apparently, was the first 'visit from outside' for a thousand years...

I continued:

'*Exoteric* comprises formal knowledge, such as theology and liturgy.

'*Intermediate* is emotional, secrecy and the like: including prayer, practices and sacramental things.

'*Esoteric* is the area wherein lies the real perception of Truth: when the individual understands what the former two aids to progress really stand for, and what Truth is.'

'Then all religions,' concluded the Priest, 'originate with the Esoteric, and are presented in the first two stages in order to make them into a teaching-system'.

I replied:

'Yes. In addition, of course, you have to know that, from time to time, the original system falters and may become extinguished, perhaps because it has fulfilled its purpose.

'But,' he asked, 'why do we not pass as a matter of course from the first to the second and then the third stage?'

I told him: 'Because the precise meaning of the third area is perceived only by realised people, whom we call Sufi Teachers. They alone can modify the first two ranges to make them properly accessible to the changing conditions of the individual learners, the mass of the community.'

The High Priest looked doleful. Then he asked me to show him some signs from his religion, and to prove that I was talking about the same thing.

'I can only show you things in the first and second range,' I said.

He eagerly agreed that that would be 'more than enough. Nobody except true Nusairis knows our hand-grips, passwords and signs.'

He seemed more depressed than ever when I gave him the hand-signals and pressures, showed him the skipping step, drew the secret symbols, and referred to colours, orientation and arrangement of their temples, and quoted from their holy book, supposedly seen by nobody from 'outside' ever before.

Why, I asked him, was he so disconsolate?

'Don't you see, Great Scholar? You know more than we do. This means that you are the root and we are the branch. We are waiting for the Messiah to come to explain the secret that we have lost. You come along and have got it, but you are not the Messiah, or even a priest. Why should I not be disconsolate?'

I had had quite a lot of experience of this kind of reaction.

'If that is all your problem is,' I told him, 'I can solve it in a couple of minutes. Just listen to me.

'In our experience, people stick to the familiar. Your people positively revel in having lost the secret. They like things to be as they are. They are trained to the first or second stages of knowledge; they may even have three or more stages which are merely symbolic: and they will settle for those. Believe me, I have seen this all before. Sufis have plenty of knowledge and information: others do not really want it. They want emotional stimulation, excitement, a sense of meaning.

'You will be able to carry on just as before, unless you wish to change.'

He fell silent, and that was the last I saw or heard of the secret sect of the Nusairis.

I was about to leave Amman for Petra and I was delighted to receive an equerry, saying that His Highness the Emir had given special orders to his military officers to escort me on my visit to Petra.

The city of the red rocks lay hidden in the heart of Arabia: a mystery rediscovered by the redoubtable German traveller Burckhardt in the nineteenth century.

When I first went there, in the early years of the twentieth century, it was no tourist spectacle, reached from London on a weekend package tour. It still retained the mystery, the strangeness, the impact, of which it was to be robbed by rubber-necked tourists.

No-one knows the origin or the prehistory of Petra; and

the scanty, earliest known records can take us back no further than the sixth century B.C.

Travelling by pony up and down the ravines of Wadi Musa, (the Valley of Moses) the terrain is no different from any encountered since leaving the fertile regions of Western Palestine – scrub wood, stunted trees, a tuft of grass here, another behind a boulder, and loose rocks mixed with grey earth.

Presently a deep valley opens and, at its mouth, a stream flows languidly. A couple of Arab women are washing their clothes in it and, according to them, it is the very same sacred spot where Moses struck the rock and water spurted out from the heart of the stone: for 'Allah had so willed it'.

Walking or riding, the path goes up and down the barren sides of the hill; gradually the dry bed of the stream opens out. Three miles more and, to the north-east, a series of curious structures comes into view.

Like small mounds of whitish grey they rise, several of them reflecting the rays of the morning sun, with shallow pits on their sides.

This is the outer range of the tombs of Petra. Now a wall of rocks rises higher and higher, rampart upon rampart shutting out everything beyond.

Presently a narrow opening in the rocks leads into a dark labyrinthine passage. Entering this, our way in the half-light is between walls of rocks, red and terra-cotta in colour. Worn smooth with age, they rise higher and higher, seeming to meet above.

At one place, the passage is so narrow that two laden camels cannot pass abreast. The voices of men seem to murmur, uncanny whispers are heard and the wind sighs like the breath of a giant dragon as it passes and echoes through the Sik, this magical passage. For nearly an hour, we continue the bewildering journey; until, rounding a sharp corner of the rocky passage, the light of the day appears as a red glow.

On closer approach the coloured glow resolves into a façade of exquisitely carved rock. This is now known as the Treasury: formerly it was a temple; and along its sides are four huge and graceful capitals.

The solid red rock is hollowed out into an enormous hall, terra-cotta sandstone showing veins of magnificent colour in its interior. The imagination boggles at the thought of the hands which fashioned such a marvel; how many years it took, how much skill . . .

Buildings these, grand and like others, impressive of the ancient world; but buildings? No, modelled on ancient temples, halls of audience, palaces they undoubtedly are: but they are not *built* – they are carved out of the living rock! That is Petra.

Further down the valley, there are rock-hewn buildings of similar grandeur on all sides. Again and again, we have to remember that these are not buildings in the ordinary sense of the word. There are no signs of *construction*; all is carved from the living, almost pulsating, rock.

Hundreds of tombs, public buildings, water tanks, temples and altars lie in their scattered glory, their history unknown; a reminder of days when the Arabian Nabateans flourished and ruled from here to Syria, finally yielding in homage to the Roman legions.

Even now in the moonlit expanse of this fairyland valley of rock carvings, one can picture the mighty warriors standing guard over the sleeping caravans on their way to distant Egypt: Or imagine the Nabateans' rain-making rites – the long procession of a Nabatean Queen wending its way up to the highest spur of the rocky defiles, where the handsomest youth of the decade was tied to the altar and married to the Queen; and then borne down on the shoulders of the priests.

In fancy, one can hear the distant neighing of the Crusaders' chargers, leaving nothing behind but three miles of carved rock which has slumbered in the heart of the desert for centuries together. Nothing but Allah remains: so much for the glory of man.

But history is one thing, and local belief is another. I camped in Petra with Abu-Zeitun, a new acquaintance and a local Bedouin. We spoke of Petra and its princes – not merely of its Roman past, the vulgar novelty of a standardizing race, but of the grey antiquity of those days when it was Selah, city of the rock, before it had been conquered by Amaziah, who gave it the unpardonably hideous name of Joktheel.

Abu-Zeitun and I smoked our water-pipes, and spoke of things unfamiliar to the Western archaeologist – things at which, indeed, those wise wizards of modern science would never guess.

We spoke for instance, of the tradition that Petra was founded by Esau, that mighty hunter of the Bible who was dispossessed by the crafty Jacob. Of the Horim, the cave-dwellers who formerly inhabited the site. And of the Nabateans who followed them, the descendants of Esau by his 'accursed' marriages with the Canaanites.

For miles on either hand stretched the extraordinary panorama of black rock, cut by the chisels of Nabatean and Roman into temple and aqueduct, arch and sculpture and votive tomb. Immediately behind me, a group of colossal figures representing centaurs were placed on each side of a portico of lofty proportions, with only a single broken column, excavated entirely from the solid rock.

I thought about the debate such an undertaking would

arouse in any Western Planning Department nowadays; arguments about unemployment, rating and working hours, and I marvelled. Would even a single column ever get produced, today?

This ancient capital of 'Stony Arabia', as Ptolemy named it, carved out of the red sandstone, has witnessed the coming and going of cave-dweller, Nabatean, Greek, Roman and Arab – and the Arab seems to be the last heir to all the civilizations of old.

But the Arab has a good memory. Bookless, he retains in his poetic mind, and perhaps in his heart, if he has one, the legends of half a dozen civilizations. Abu-Zeitun was typical in this regard: he seemed to remember almost every grain in the bags of fodder with which he supplied my horses, and the market-price of millet in Aden. He well remembered the legend of Petra, a legend no European has yet set down in writing.

Petra is more dry and desiccated than Texas; its community's entire existence has always depended upon the rain-clouds which cluster round the peak of Mount Sinai, the ancient seat of the thunder-god of the Semites.

The cult and mystery of the Nabateans was associated almost entirely with the making of rain. In their naive philosophy, only one thing could conjure down the amount of moisture necessary to the growth of the millet: necessary to their very survival.

Abu-Zeitun closed his eyes, almost in a reverie, and I guessed that he was trying to recollect an ancient story current amongst his Bedouin folk.

At last he opened his eyes, and as if impelled suddenly by some inward emotion: 'Listen!' he burst out. 'A strange tale is told of one of those princesses who ruled in Petra in the time of the Nabateans.

'You should know that a year after their unwholesome

135

rites, the Princess ceased to rule the city and could then marry whom she pleased.

'One such lady, whose name was Ashtar, was wed to a certain noble a year after the horrid ordeal but, after the manner of some women, she cast her eyes on another, and longed to be free of that husband she had taken to herself. And quickly her evil mind discovered a manner of doing so.

'A plague fell upon the valley, and for some moons the rain had not fallen at its proper time. The furious heat and parched soil caused a dreadful distemper of the throat, and thousands perished.

'Then came this evil princess to the judges, and said that a sacrifice was necessary to the god of thunder. The judges of the people answered that the usual rites had been performed, and that never in the history of the city had they been repeated.

'But this wicked woman, her heart set upon another, told them that she had had a dream or vision in which the god had appeared to her. He had commanded that she be set in the place of the princess who had succeeded her, and once more bound to the pillars along with the wretched man, her husband, who should be sacrificed to the demon-god.

And so mightily were the judges carried away by her eloquence and so furiously did the people rage for a victim that without delay they took her and seized the man, her husband, and bound them to the pillars.

'But scarcely had they done so when the heavens opened and a frightful peal of thunder crashed above the city. A shaft of lightning descended like a red lance, and striking that evil woman, slew her in an instant.

'Then came the rain, torrents of it, until the valley seemed like a river, and the people, terrified, sought refuge in the caves and tombs above. Again the lightning descended, but this time onto the pillar to which the husband of that devilish witch had been bound, burning through his bonds and setting him free.'

8

The Shrine

Worn out with roaming about amongst the rock caves and tombs of Petra followed by an evening of story-telling with Abu-Zeitun, I slept the sleep of the weary: in, of all places, that enormous stone hall called the Treasury. It had probably been a temple of Isis, reputed to have been built by Hadrian in AD 131.

Outside, my companions and guide were loading my baggage onto pack ponies: I took the opportunity to enjoy a last look at the façade of that remarkable edifice. Its two storeys – about 65 feet high – were carved onto the face of living red stone. Four columns of the first storey were broken; but the two central ones were complete and a delight to the eye: the skilled workmanship in those cornices and pediments was amazing.

Soon we were winding our way back through the long narrow Sik, away from the caves and palaces and tombs of this lost city of the desert. The rock walls rose as high as one hundred and fifty feet to either side and there were niches here and there for horsemen to pass; and a clay water pipe could still be seen embedded in a form of cement.

Passing obelisks, rock tombs and sanctuaries, we returned to the Wadi Musa: the Valley of Moses. With the rock mountains of Petra behind us, we jogged along stony ground, until we reached the village of Elji.

From there I took the road to Mecca – though there are no roads as such in this desert part of the country, as the West understands the word. Here I joined a caravan of pilgrims going southwards towards Mecca, by way of the Gulf of Akaba on the Red Sea, where Jordan's only seaport is located.

This land is bleak and forlorn; empty but for the occasional pilgrims' caravan. As we went southwards, day after day, we traversed wadi after dry wadi wherein nothing grew, nothing lived. Here and there, we came upon the ruins of Roman forts, or of caravanserais or perhaps a khan. On and onward we pressed.

Once during this journey, our path lay along a Roman road. On it was a shrine near the crossing point between the pilgrim routes, a little beyond the Wadi Yetem, and our caravan-leader decided to camp near it. The most remarkable thing about the building was that a fair-sized village had sprung up around it. The offerings of the pilgrims had been considerable at times.

This was one of those tombs which dot the path of pilgrimages and are often popular elements in the homage of prayer which constitutes the merit of the devout.

In or near each of the most important, many devotees feel that at least one night's watch must be spent. The more precise in his prayers the pilgrim, the greater the degree of religious experience he will expect from the sacred recesses.

This one in which I now found myself was a place of peculiar sanctity, the tomb of a tribal patriarch of exceeding virtue, plain and in no wise spacious, yet with something in its atmosphere of brooding sanctity which only tradition and long association can give.

The grey-domed interior was packed with pilgrims after sunset, and soon the temperature of the shrine had become overpowering in its sweaty heat.

The droning recital of long passages from the Koran, the pious exclamations, the muttered prayers, had a soporific effect. The walls began to drip with moisture, the packed bodies could scarcely find space for their continual prostrations and genuflections.

After the free air of the desert, the closeness became intolerable. I began to realise why Ibn Saud, in Arabia to the south, had forcibly banned the use of all such shrines. Yet no-one seemed to be paying any attention to the discomfort, raised and exalted as they were in an experience of perfervid piety and straining after what they took to be the divine.

At times a prolonged hush would fall upon the assembled company, which seemed rich and intimate with holy consideration, the deep conviction of generations as to the reality of the Spirit of God. The night, indeed, seemed not of today or yesterday. Free of the trammels of time, it was almost an hour in eternity, set apart from calendars or seasons.

Suddenly, startlingly, out of the silence would rise the voice of an old man strident in the accents of prayer. A profound, resonant monotone, the very fibre of which seemed eloquent of that ancient patriarchal emphasis in which the East is still so rich, despite all the influence of modernity. Thus Abraham might have addressed his God in the cave of Macpelah. To hear such an ancient was to understand the whole rugged past of the desert. The long struggle against paganism and infidelity, the certainty that righteousness would prevail, that indeed it was the only pillar to which one might cleave in a sinful world, the very roof-tree of the human being's house.

A great murmur of response would arise again and again at the words: like a sad and mournful wind, rising to the little dome which threw it back in hollow and chorus-like echo.

I cannot hope to convey in words the total conviction present. When man is so caught up in rapture, any words which seek to picture his state, must seem as things cold and counterfeit, set beside the experience which I witnessed that night.

There was another shrine not far from Akaba, which although now desolate and of little account to the discerning, still received a few offerings from marauding gangs of Bedouins of the desert – the Shrine of The Unknown One.

Its history, as faithfully related to me, should be a lesson to us all – especially the more credulous of shrine-hunters.

The Keeper of the Shrine was named Aziz.

During his occupancy, the place had grown in fame as a centre for the cure of all kinds of diseases. Pilgrims visited it from far and near; the well-meaning sat in meditation before the shrine to purify their souls; the childless tied little bits of red rags to its bushes so as to be blessed with children, and the blind had offered gifts to have their eyesight restored; Aziz sat mute, collecting the offerings.

One Sulaiman, his devoted disciple, attended to all the wants of the old man. He looked after Aziz's sleeping quarters in an alcove, he prepared his meals; and, on holy days, he washed his master's feet, in the usual Eastern token of respect.

Sulaiman gave years of service and asked for no reward, other than a small share of the rice which the Faithful brought for the use of the priest.

He was a true ascetic, and dear to the old man's heart. Then, one day Aziz, fell ill. He thought that he was dying.

Sulaiman cared for him, and nursed him back to health. The illness, however, caused the old man to think somewhat of the future. He addressed his faithful disciple.

'Sulaiman,' he said, 'the time has come when we must think beyond the present.'

Sulaiman knelt, and touched the old man's feet with his hands.

'Rise, my son,' said Aziz, 'you have been a good and devoted servant of the shrine, and I – I am getting old. The time will be when I must nominate a successor. You Sulaiman, have shown yourself to be worthy.'

Sulaiman made a double obeisance. 'Master,' he said, deeply affected, 'I am unworthy.'

'That will not always be,' went on the sage. 'To qualify yourself and to attain that level of sanctity which is incumbent upon him who would cherish the shrine, you must do even as I. You must depart from here. You must scour the highways and byways, and you must live on that which is offered. You must travel from shrine to shrine, meditating long at each. Gradually you will attain that eminence of thought which creates the saint from the dross of the mere mortal. You will yourself know when that time comes. Then return here – and at that time you shall inherit the shrine.'

'Master!' breathed Sulaiman, once more.

'You will walk abroad, as I did,' proceeded the master. 'As a mark of special favour, you may carry the staff which assisted me on my lengthy journeys. And,' ended the old man, with heavy emphasis upon this valuable gift, 'in order to have a link with me here, you shall have my old donkey. On your travels, walk until you are fatigued. Only then may you mount my donkey, for he is old, like me.'

So Sulaiman departed on his wanderings, with the staff

143

and the donkey as his companions. He regarded the stick with reverence, but the animal he placed upon a plane above all things. He cared for it as he had cared for the old man.

Often he went hungry that it might eat, and when passing through the sandy places of the desert, he frequently subsisted on the minimum of water so that the donkey might drink its fill. Never once did he attempt to ride it, no matter how long the trek. He associated the animal with the shrine and its holy custodian. He regarded the beast with veneration.

Months later, Sulaiman had crossed both desert and high mountain passes. He came to the wilds of desolate mountains, and then emerged onto the desert once more. Often he was in bad straits, for charitable offerings were scarce, and the waterholes were few and far between.

However he persisted in his quest – the attainment of that degree of moral elevation which would qualify him for the life's work that awaited him in the distant desert village of his origins.

The way was hard, both for man and donkey, and it was the donkey that gave out first. As the saint had said, it was old, very old.

For days it had dragged its footsteps, its long ears drooping wearily over its great, over-heavy head. Then, right off the caravan-route and miles from any sort of sustenance, far from its homeland and its original master, it crashed to the ground, dead.

Sulaiman was beside himself with grief. To him the animal was much more than a donkey. It represented almost everything dear and sacred to him.

In his misery he only gazed at the carcase before him and thought little of his own plight. When he looked up he saw, far off, tiny black dots in the sky. They were the vultures, waiting – ready to descend when he continued on his way.

He resolved that his old friend should not become carrion. Frenziedly, he scooped at the sand with his hands and made a shallow depression. Then he dragged the donkey into it and raised sand upon its body. It made a mound.

He sank down exhausted after his efforts and at last gave consideration to his own plight. Wearily, his head between his hands, he sat there for hours waiting for inspiration to guide his footsteps.

He was roused by a distant sound. He gazed into the direction from which it came and made out an approaching body of horsemen. They could help him. He was saved.

As the horsemen approached, he began to have qualms. He was there in the desert with what was unmistakably a grave. He pondered his dilemma.

If he told the men of the cavalcade that he had buried a donkey, they would think him mad. Failing that, they would disbelieve him and declare that it was the body of a man whom he had probably murdered. If he told them that it was the body of a man, they would be inquisitive in their questioning, and they would trip him up. And, these men of the desert were very ready with their knives. It was an uncomfortable prospect.

The riders came nearer and still he was undecided on his course of action. One of the men detached himself from the party and cantered towards Sulaiman.

'What ails you, friend?' he demanded. 'Our Sheikh would have speech with you.'

Unable to formulate an answer, Sulaiman bowed his head.

The rider looked around, first at the mound and then at the disciple. Accustomed to making quick judgements, he took in the situation.

'I observe your grief, brother,' he said sympathizing. 'I can see that you are a disciple, probably of an aged one, and have lost your leader. The ancient creature of Allah has been overcome by the rigours of the desert.'

'Aye!' responded Sulaiman brokenly.

The man wheeled away and conferred with his Sheikh. The entire body of horsemen then came towards Sulaiman. Stopping a short distance away, the Sheikh himself dismounted and approached the distracted figure.

'Holy man,' he said, 'I observe you mourning at the grave of your venerated companion. The grief which you display tells me that he was a good and saintly one. My men will supply you with food and water. Remain here as long as you need for your prayers and meditations. I, paramount Sheikh of this entire territory, will see that you come to no harm.'

Sulaiman could do no more than gaze at the mound.

The Sheikh departed, and he kept his promise. A regular supply of food was forthcoming. Also, his men searched until they found a site for a well.

The men, beholding Sulaiman crouching by the mound, mistook his mental lethargy for profound meditation. Some of them brought dried flowers from a distant oasis, and placed them on the mound. Then they planted gardens, watered by the abundant well. A tree grew from the staff which Sulaiman had stuck in the ground, and was soon regarded as miraculous.

Gradually, the story spread far and wide. The exceedingly holy man sitting out in the desert was under the protection of the Sheikh. He remained faithfully dedicated, at the site of his great and illustrious leader, a man

146

of the greatest possible sanctity. People brought sweets, fruit and money as offerings to the holy man.

Sulaiman remained. His inspiration was yet to come. Meanwhile, the number and quantity of the offerings increased. Before he quite realized it, he found that he was the guardian of a shrine. He wrestled long with his conscience and would have told the truth, but things had gone too far. Those who came to pray at the shrine would never believe him, especially if he told them that the mound covered the earthly remains of an ass.

The fame of the shrine grew. There were those who declared that it was endowed with great healing power. There were others, who said that the custodian was strong in prayer and was, indeed, a very holy man. They could feel it as they stood in his presence, could they not?

Eventually, the fame of the shrine spread across the entire desert and even over the mountains, until those pilgrims who visited the other shrine, that of Aziz, had heard of its sanctity.

Some of them by-passed the shrine of Aziz and made the lengthy journey to that of Sulaiman.

They returned with stories which enhanced the popularity of Sulaiman's shrine.

Others followed in their footsteps. The flow of coins into the bowl before the old sage in the desert village near Akaba gradually dwindled, almost to vanishing-point.

This worried the old man, for he was attached to his shrine, yet there was little that he could do. He realized that he now had a very strong rival. His offerings grew ever less, until they were confined to those proffered by the local people.

The old man, after much thought, decided to visit the distant shrine. It was a long and wearisome journey for old Aziz, but he was determined to find out how such a very new tomb could beat his in sanctity. After all, he had been guardian of his own shrine for nearly two score years and three before he reached the top of his profession.

After many hardships, he reached the shrine whose competition had, effectively, put him out of business.

Aziz made obeisance before the now heavily-shrouded, long-bearded figure of the custodian of the new shrine, even as other pilgrims were bending low before Sulaiman.

A voice he knew well came softly to him.

'Do you not know me, Master?' it said. 'Do you not observe Sulaiman, your disciple behind this beard?'

The old man trembled and looked again. 'It is indeed, Sulaiman,' and, after a long pause, 'Sulaiman, who left me to attain spiritual elevation.'

'Master, master; I have much to tell you. I have a confession to make, one which can be made only to you.' Sulaiman bowed his head in his distress.

'I have long awaited for this moment,' he went on, his voice betraying his agitation. 'There is so much on my conscience. And only you can know, Master. There is no one else who can relieve me of my burden.'

'My son, what is it?' Aziz asked gently.

Half-weeping, Sulaiman told his story: 'The shrine which you see here, and which folk believe to be endowed with such holiness,' he sobbed, 'this tomb to which thousands of pilgrims come to make their offerings, which is shortly to be replaced by a huge marble sepulchre – it contains nothing more than the body of your dead donkey!'

The old sage pulled at his beard, and ruminated.

'What can I do, Master? What can I do?' Sulaiman broke in.

Still the old man pondered.

'Master?'

The old man stirred. He gazed gravely at Sulaiman. 'I am now very old,' he said, 'and the world is ever-changing. Your shrine here has transcended in popularity even that which is in our desert village. The offerings at my shrine have dwindled – gone!'

'Master!'

'It is well.' The old man was impressive. He retained that gaze that fixes men. Then he spoke again.

'It is as well, Sulaiman, that you should not have asked me much beyond your daily prayer whilst at the other shrine, and let the matter rest at that. I am most infirm now and shall reside with you here, until, soon, my days are over.

'But know, my son, know the truth at last. The shrine which I tended for forty-three years was none other than the resting-place of the bones of a donkey! And that animal was the father of the one which you have enshrined here.'

'Yes, Master,' breathed Sulaiman in amazement and relief, 'I understand.'

Descending from the Wadi Yetam, our caravan had yet to traverse a plain before reaching Akaba, and the heat was overpowering. It was therefore decided to pitch the tents in the plain for the night.

Not far off was a desert sheikh's encampment. Hearing that at least some of us were pilgrims, he promptly invited us all to share his board; or, rather, his table-cloth spread on a priceless Persian rug.

I did not think that I would be able to attend, for my immediate need was water. My pony had not had a drop for more than thirty-eight hours. Where we had halted, the rest of the animals had taken all the water from the wells and it would be days before the ooze replenished them.

I searched for another water-hole. A Bedouin guide indicated three heaps of stones some two miles distant, marking the sites of wells. The only one which I was able to reach before nightfall was more or less choked with sand. What little water there was could only be obtained by lowering down a battered leather bucket and then raising it again, full of salty, fairly brackish water.

With this, I served my mount as best as I could; he relished it: and I was in time for dinner with the Sheikh.

Sheikh Hamoud was a powerfully-built man, who sat surrounded by my companions from the caravan. He was interested and relieved to hear that we had had no encounters with roving gangs of raiding Bedouins who were in the locality.

Outside the low black tent where we sat, the sandy waste stretched till it met the stark rocks of the Akaba hills beyond. Nothing was stirring, nothing moved except the Sheikh's camels being brought back to the encampment from the watering-holes. The entire plain was dipped in the golden light of the setting sun.

After the meal, Sheikh Hamoud regaled us with the stories of the desert; but the one which I found most enthralling was a tale involving Prince Malik Nasir of Egypt, from whom the Sheikh traced his ancestry.

That there was such a person as Malik Nasir in Egyptian history is known well enough, but it puzzled me how he could have escaped the wrath of his brother, the ruler, into the land of Sinai and thence to Baghdad, with his descendants spread out in the desert here.

'By Allah, you don't believe me!' roared the Sheikh, when I ventured to show surprise; 'I shall recite you the ballad which tells of the Prince from whom we are descended.'

Since I was a guest, he was dealing leniently with me: for it is killing-talk to question anyone's ancestry among the desert Arabs.

Eight men took turns to recite the Nasirian family saga, with no detail excluded, however trivial; until I, at least, was sorry we had accepted his hospitality. By the time the recitation finished, it was well past midnight, and we had each drunk more than eighteen cups of coffee.

It all related to Prince Nasir who, as a political refugee, is said to have joined anonymously, a pilgrim caravan on its way to Mecca.

On the way a rich doctor lost a purse containing his savings. This pouch the disguised prince had found and given back intact to its owner. The Doctor, being a devout man, promised that he would pray to Allah for the honest pilgrim when they were facing the Great Shrine, the Merciful Kaaba in the Mecca mosque.

He prayed hard and fervently; and then invited the disguised prince to accompany him to his home in Baghdad where he practised the art of healing.

So rare is the story that I have set it down in the Sheikh's own words:

'When they had arrived in Baghdad, the Prince, my illustrious ancestor, said to the Doctor: "Doctor, I do not wish to be an expense to you. I can make clothes as well as any man: please recommend me to some tailor of your acquaintance."

'The Doctor placed him with the most noted tailor in the city; who, to try his new lad, gave him cloth to cut out and make a suit of clothes.

'Malik Nasir, who had excited the admiration of the master-tailors of Cairo with the results of his hobby, could not fail to succeed in the less sophisticated Baghdad. He made a suit of clothes, which his master liked so well that he showed it to all the other tailors of the city, who confessed that it was a masterpiece of their art.

'The tailor was well satisfied to have so expert a journeyman, and he paid him well, so that Nasir had enough to live handsomely in Baghdad.

'This was the Prince's condition, when one day the Doctor, Abu Yunus, who was a man of ungovernable temper, fell out with his wife, and, in the heat of his anger, said to her: "Be gone! once, twice, thrice, I repudiate thee."

'Although legal and binding, such a repudiation is against Islamic injunctions. He had no sooner pronounced these words than he repented of them, for he loved his wife; nay, he would have kept her in his house, and lived with her as before. He consulted the judge, who opposed this, saying that a *khala* must lie with her first; that is to say, another man must first marry, and then divorce her. After that, the Doctor might marry her again if he pleased. That was the law.

'The Doctor, seeing himself under a necessity to submit to the law, resolved to take Prince Malik Nasir – or, rather, his friend the honest pilgrim-tailor – for his khala.

'"I had best," he said to himself, "take for a khala this young man whom I brought from Mecca to Baghdad; he is a foreigner, and an honest fellow; I can make him do what I will. He shall marry my wife tonight and tomorrow I will have him divorce her."

'Having taken this resolution, he sent for her and Nasir, had them married in front of witnesses, and left them in a chamber together.

'The lady, however, had no sooner set her eyes on Malik Nasir than she fell in love with him. The Prince, for his part, liked her very much. They revealed their thoughts to each other, and neglected not to give one another all the proofs of mutual affection that the place and opportunity afforded them.

'After the expression of many reciprocal feelings, the lady showed the Prince several caskets full of gold, silver, and jewels.

'"Know thou," said she, "that all these riches belong to me! This is the cabinet, that is to say, the portion, that I brought the Doctor. By divorcing me he was obliged by law to restore them to me, and I now possess them again.

'"If you will declare tomorrow, that you will not part with me, but keep me for your lawful wife, you shall be master of all this, and of my person."

'"Since it is so," replied Malik Nasir, "I promise you I will not part with you: you are young, beautiful and rich. I might chance to make a worse choice. When the Doctor comes, you shall see how I will receive him."

'Very early the next morning the Doctor opened the door, and came into the chamber. The Prince met him halfway into the room with a smile upon his lips, and said:

'"Doctor, I am obliged to you for having helped me to so charming a wife!"

'"Young man," answered the Doctor, "turn towards her, and say: 'Be gone! once, twice, thrice, I divorce thee.' "

'"I should be very sorry to do that," replied Malik Nasir. "It is a great crime in my country for a man to repudiate his wife. It is an ignominious action, and husbands that are so base as to be guilty of it are reproached with it as long as they live. Since I have married this lady, I will of course keep her."

'"Ai, ai! young man," said the Doctor, "what means this language? You do but jest with me!"

'"No, Doctor," answered the Prince, "I speak the truth. I find the lady to my mind. Please think no more of her, for it would be to no purpose."

'"O Heaven!" cried the Doctor. "What a khala have I chosen? How prone are men to be mistaken in their judgments! Alas! I had rather he had kept my purse, than that he should keep my wife."

'The Prince continued so firm that the Doctor, losing every prospect of altering his resolution by fair means, went to the judge to complain of the khala.

'The judge only laughed at his complaints, declaring that the lady was no longer his: that she lawfully belonged to the young tailor; and that he could not be compelled to divorce her.

'The Doctor fell into despair at this adventure. His misfortune told upon his health: he became ill and the malady progressed from bad to worse.

'When his end drew nigh he desired to speak with the Prince. "Young man," he confided, "I forgive you for detaining my wife; I ought not to take it ill of you; it was the Will of Allah that it should be so. You remember that I prayed for you in the shrine at Mecca?"

'"Yes," said the Prince, "and I remember, besides, that I heard not one word of all your prayer, though I heartily said amen – I knew not to what."

'"Hear then," replied the Doctor, "what were the words of my supplication:- O my God! let all my estate, and all I hold dear, become one day the lawful portion of this excellent, this honest, this superb young man . . ."

'You realise, therefore,' the Sheikh now reminded us, 'that I am not only a sheikh. I am aware, as you will also be, that among the true desert Arabs, "Sheikh" is the only title which exists: except perhaps Emir, which only means

"He who is in command". But, through my descent from Nasir, I am also a royal prince, a Malik in my own right.'

The story of the Sheikh's ancestry may or may not have been correct, but reclining in his tent against the saddles of camels and on hay mattresses, certainly gave my tired bones a rest. I wished however, that the story could have been related with greater brevity and less poetical garnishing of the verses, which occurred frequently during its well-rehearsed flow.

As the moon rose, we bade good-bye to the Sheikh. While I walked towards our own encampment, where I was to sleep upon the hard, stony ground with only a blanket as my bed, I looked up and saw the huge, yellow face of the moon – smiling on the dark and dense walls of the Akaba hills, now only a day's march away.

Next day, we entered Akaba by way of the large entrance gate with its two towers. The rest-house for pilgrims swallowed us. Here too, I detached myself from the other pilgrims going on south-east, for I wanted to meet another sheikh in this neighbourhood.

This sheikh sought those who hungered after adventure. I had been told by those who had enlisted me for 'human service' that the nature of the adventure would be revealed to me if and when I passed his scrutiny.

While I waited for the Sheikh's summons, I had a look at the old town.

Even as desert towns, or should I say villages go, Akaba was a disappointing place: mud huts, some orchards, a port of sorts. Undeveloped, it was then only of interest to Judeo-Christians because nearby is the Elath of scripture.

Some of its inhabitants were reputed to possess a letter from the Prophet Mohammed, and I was actually shown a grotto wherein the letter was kept for some time; as a Holy Sanctuary. As to what happened to it, and whether there was indeed a letter of that kind, no authentic record exists. The only importance that the town had was that it lay on the pilgrim route to Mecca, and here I was to meet the Sheikh who set me a strange task.

9

The Dope-Smugglers

Sheikh Jasim, outlining my programme of work, suggested my first of all tasting opium. His manner was so ingratiating, his reasoning so apparently logical, that I almost found myself complying.

Suddenly, however, common-sense began to assert itself, even if only in a slightly confused way. Here was my superior officer, in the struggle against habit-forming drugs, trying to get me to indulge. Had he himself been compromised, or was this just a test?

Besides, there was the matter of my upbringing. Narcotics, it had always been drummed into me, were one of the greatest dangers to humanity on earth ... And my training in Beirut.

I could discern nothing from his face. I simply said, loudly, 'No!'

'But Sidi,' he insisted, 'you misunderstand. If you are to help us track down the drug-smugglers, you must know all about these substances, even ... even about their effects on your own system.'

I said nothing, and neither did he.

'You leave it to me, O Sheikh,' I replied at last. 'There will be enough time for such experience when I know

157

more about drugs, and have worked with your people a bit longer.'

'All right, then,' he said; 'we'll leave it until later. I'll put that in my report on you.

'And there,' he said pointing to something that looked like a slight discoloured patch in the sea lapping upon the coastline in the distance, 'shall you see the boat – the boat – ' He grinned.

Yes, the drug ship; we were, of course, both on the same side: but I couldn't say that I liked him, exactly. I suppose, with hindsight, that it was immaturity and the prospect of my first undercover mission – *Inshallah* – if Allah wills! that made me think that all allies should be friends.

The Nubian servant now placed a coffee-pot before the Sheikh. From it, he poured not two cups of coffee, but of delicious saffron-coloured tea. I had become attached to it in Central Asia. Perhaps he had got that fact from my dossier . . .

The tea, too, had just the right aroma of cardamom.

That a Sharqi – an Eastern Arab – should break the tradition of his people by drinking not coffee but tea, because his guest preferred that beverage, and that he knew about my preference, seemed a high tribute to myself, and I said so to the Sheikh.

He smiled benignly, and motioned me to drink.

Then a thought leapt into my mind. I fished out my small bottle of smelling salts. My host and superior officer said that he was sorry that I had headache. He thought that the tea would do me more good than my remedy.

But a sneeze shook my hand, and a few crystals of the salts dropped into the cup. Presently, as the Sheikh looked on irascibly, I stirred the tea. It was as I had expected: it lost its transparency. Ammonia, when mixed with an aqueous solution of opium, turns it cloudy . . .

I merely looked hard at the Sheikh.

He spoke next: 'Your first battle is won, Sidi,' he smiled, 'you should do well, all right. Only a test, you understand.'

The Sheikh played no more tricks on me for the next three days while I stayed with him waiting for the ship's arrival. Nor did he come to the jetty to see me off, for he would have probably laughed at my artificial beard. As it was, two of the sailors on the gangway looked suspiciously at my innocent canvas holdall and basket of dates.

Just behind our cargo ship sailed a great liner. Several first class passengers came to the rail and peered regally down on me, discussing the quaint, hairy native squatting on the deck. I wondered whether they knew of the drug traffic and what people, even miserable natives, had to risk to fight it.

Two Indians who had got on the boat at the same time as me were busy washing their loincloths in the lee of a lifeboat – a corner allotted to us, the lowly deck passengers – when a sailor came to say that the captain wanted to see me.

As I entered his cabin, I could have leapt for joy. Instead of finding only one of the arch-smugglers there, in the person of the villainous Dimitrios whom I was expecting, there were three more whose ill-repute equalled his.

Not for nothing had I gazed on their photographs for days, memorising their every feature. Now one quick glance was enough to show that the whole of a powerful and much-sought gang was there.

'So you think that you are very clever?' huskily asked Dimitrios, in almost comically accented English. The captain's tunic cast aside over a torn and dirty chair in that miserable cabin, he looked every inch a high priest of smugglers.

'Speak!' he thundered.

'My wits are confounded, sir,' I replied in assumed innocence. 'Perhaps you are thinking of someone who looks like me?'

He grimaced and threw me a copy of the coded telegram which I had received only two hours before boarding his vessel. There was no further point in lying, and I admitted to being an investigator.

Threatening him with the usual penalties, and knowing that I was probably for the high jump, I asked him what he proposed to do with me.

'Do with you?' growled one of the other Greek ruffians, 'boil you in oil, slowly: except that oil is too precious for cooking dogs in!'

Now our information was that Dimitrios's crew were on the point of mutiny. He was not only a hard taskmaster, but a bad payer too. At times he would even take a lash to his stokers, which is the one of the most serious crimes among seamen.

He had been putting off his men by saying that when he had 'cargo' – meaning opium – from three more ports, and was successful in getting the stuff over to Italy, everybody would be well paid.

The plan was to use his haste to help trap his entire gang, who would be supplying him with 'cargo' at various points upto Suez. That was why I was on the boat.

Of course, if I had had any means of communicating with the coastal police, I could have cut the job short; but I did not, and Dimitrios had other plans.

He did not now need to touch at any intermediate ports before Suez, where he was to receive something like seven hundred kilos of raw opium. From earlier ports of call, he already had nearly two hundred kilos.

After some discussion, the gang decided that I might be

useful as a hostage if and when they came upon unbribable officials. For the time being, rather than kill me they had merely flung me amongst the peanut bags, loads of hides and of course, the canvas opium sacks.

The heat in the hold, the stench and the darkness were all but unbearable; with rats and other vermin as my only companions in the hold, for days on end.

But those who have had similar experiences of acute mental and physical distress will know that, given a fair degree of confidence in the mission, the awfulness of the plight sharpens that peculiar sense in the brain which works out possible means of escape with remarkable clarity.

My mind, therefore, was not at all dull, nor were my limbs and teeth. I had planned a single-handed attack, a way to get hold of a revolver and ammunition: and my teeth, gnawing incessantly at the rope around my wrists and feet, had given me freedom. Even my two artificial teeth had worked, mercifully and gallantly, for the common good.

I reckoned it pretty smart work to get out of the hold: especially for one fed on weak pea soup and bad fish for four days. Now my lunging at the armed Sudanese guard in the galley so terrified him in the half-light that, instead of drawing his revolver, he stared at me as if he were seeing a ghost.

Then, gathering his wits, he heaved his giant bulk towards me. I ducked, and his chin very luckily cracked on the iron bars of the companion-way. His weapon now being in my possession, I pretended that I had a confederate from among the crew with me, who was covering us from a corner, and so managed quite easily to gag him and tie him up.

As I climbed up out of the bowels of the ship, the faint

sound of exotic, Eastern music struck my ears. Crawling on my belly, disorientated and weakened from lack of food, I felt as if I was being drawn towards that slow, soft sound.

Then a woman's voice burst into song; there was all the mystery of the sea, and of the East, in that voice. I drew nearer and nearer, as does a cobra to its charmer, and peered through a chink in the saloon door.

The Greek bully was asleep, slipping off his chair, and his three companions were none too wakeful either; yet the girl sang on.

I lay down on the deck as one lost in a dream, forgetting that we had entered the Suez Canal.

Soon we would be nearing Ismailia, which lies on the last lake before Port Said; and Ismailia was to be the point of our attack on these robbers of the world's souls.

Trembling again, the girl's voice rose, creeping through the hushed air, blending with the whispering of the calm sea, with the full moon of well past midnight laughing over it all.

And the singer! The Houris of Paradise, the 'Creatures of Light', I thought, mesmerised, must be like unto her.

Her long jet-black hair, her sparkling eyes; her arching eyebrows meeting like twin scimitars. Oh, Allah, I sighed, such beauty amongst such villains! Again the paradox . . . The enchanted music must have made me drowsy. Undoubtedly it sent me to sleep.

An instant's rude awakening came upon me, as I felt a heavy blow upon my head. I fell amongst a myriad stars.

'Slosh a little brandy into the dog's mouth! Don't pet the bastard!' was the gracious remark with which my ears were assailed as I woke to consciousness. Cool and fragrant fingers, the woman singer's, were fixing a dressing upon my brow.

Now she bent over me, and I could smell her perfumed robes of red, finest silk. I let the spirits trickle down my cheeks; not a drop would I let through compressed lips. Dimitrios kicked me into a sitting position.

'Now,' he asked, 'what is your price? Tell us the Agency's plans, and you can have a partnership in a good business, or . . .'

He stroked the revolver which I had held before beginning to moon over the music.

'Talk!' shouted another smuggler. I knew that death was really near; and dying men are desperate.

'Give me your knife! I'll cut his throat!' roared Dimitrios, meaning business, but the other fellow refused, saying that he did not wish his knife polluted by dog's blood. He suggested that I would co-operate with them if I were made an addict.

I was given my first fix, bound hand and foot, and then made to swallow a horrid liquid, in which was dissolved some opium.

When two knives are pushed between one's teeth; one is pulled up and the other down, and the head is held down, swallowing becomes a necessity. I felt that I would die choking, especially when my nostrils were pinched.

It was not much fun to see the four of them eyeing me with interest whilst the drug took effect.

I asked for some water to drink, for I was getting thirsty beyond measure. They gave me all I wanted – but still I drank more. Slowly the fatigue which had been overpowering me lessened. My head was clearing. I began to blink my eyes and it felt as if a cloud was being lifted from my very being. Then I had a ticklish sensation, as if a spider had started to run up and down my spine.

Now I was smiling. A remarkable happiness stole upon me. I actually began to think kindly of those four fiends whom I would willingly have slain a few minutes ago. I felt that they were really very nice people. I must have mumbled something expressive of my increasing friendliness towards them, for Dimitrios himself lumbered up with a chair, and then helped me on to a shake-down divan.

My imagination began to brighten. I could have written poetry and I felt at peace with the world. Then my eyelids became heavy – and finally I sank into the sleep of the dead.

Next day, I awoke with a start and found myself still in the saloon. It was just noon by the clock. Although my hands and feet were still tied up, I felt extraordinarily well.

Time to do some thinking!

The only other person in the room was the girl, who took up her guitar and began singing, seemingly unconcerned about what was going on around her.

This time, however, I was not inclined to be too romantic, and asked her for some water. My brain was making plans again.

Whether the bowl slipped out of her hand, or what befell, is of little import to the reader, but it so happened that I tripped her up and my hands found her throat.

She did my bidding and cut the cord from my limbs, with an ornamental but sharp knife which dangled from a hook on the wall. Once again, I was in possession of a weapon. I tied her up, barred the door of the saloon, and waited; those were awful moments.

My orders were that these smugglers were to be caught dead or alive and I was determined to take no more risks. It seemed to be a question of either shooting them, or of being killed myself.

There was no point in simply capturing the opium, for the smugglers could afford to lose the consignment and ply their trade elsewhere, provided they saved their precious skins. Hereabouts, smuggling narcotics carried an automatic death penalty.

If they were able to save even a small proportion of their opium, they could still get a huge sum for each pound sold: and still more if the stuff could be transported to morphine factories in Sicily and elsewhere. From there, its final destination would be the streets of London, where colossal fortunes could be amassed.

Two injections of heroin to each person could be all that were needed to start the vicious circle for ever. If the physical addiction does not appear, the psychological craving can do the job.

With all this in mind, and Ismailia by now well within view, I reckoned that any shooting by the crooks would be heard, and help forthcoming. So I thought to force the issue and did not have long to wait: soon there were angry voices outside the saloon door.

'Open the door, Salama!' shouted Dimitrios in broken Arabic, rattling the handle.

No reply came from the girl, as I had gagged her; nor did I speak.

'Open this door!' boomed the other Greek, in fractured French.

I said, in Greek, that Salama was resting, and it was not convenient to open the door.

'And who the devil are you?' asked the furious and confused Dimitrios.

'Satan himself,' I replied. I had found my revolver and it was ready for action. They swore that they would send me to the home of the devil: and set their shoulders against the none-too-secure door. With the first mighty heave it gave way, and their bodies came hurtling in.

I let them have it with my gun – whoever fell, I cared

not. Later, I realised that I had wounded innocent crew-members, who had been offered gold to kill me.

Climbing over prostrate bodies, I forced my way into the blazing sunlight and flattened myself behind a hatch-cover as Dimitrios, clutching his side, aimed erratic shots at me.

Then there was a stampede, for a police launch was steaming towards us, and one of our light aircraft droned in the distance, a huge floodlight already switched on.

Dimitrios was working overtime, shouting to the Sudanese and some other sailors to lower a boat. In his panic, I was relieved to note that he had left off chasing me.

When the rescue party arrived however, my 'face was blackened' as the Persians say: we could find neither the three smugglers in the boat – nor were there any drugs.

We searched the ship several times without finding a trace of what we wanted. Of the miscreants, only the woman remained, lying motionless, a gaping wound in her chest.

But the head of the rescue party had grown grey in the ways of the drug traffickers before, having reformed, he had joined ADI, Anti-Drug Intelligence. He advised us to wait till dusk, and allowed the boat to proceed on its way in the charge of other officials.

Sure enough just before midnight, from our hiding place among the reeds of an island, we saw black shadows dipping into the water from the opposite bank. They were hauling something towards the shore.

We gave chase in our motor launch and found that the men were reclaiming the large canvas bags of opium which had been thrown overboard during the excitement earlier that day.

After a good deal of forceful persuasion, the captured

men informed us that the three chief smugglers were, even then, hiding across the water.

It took time to mount a hunt for those three men. Not that we did not know the danger of giving the smugglers half a night's start, but it was necessary to get cars with balloon tyres which do not sink in soft sand. With the three cars we sped into to the Sinai desert.

By midday, we had found no trace and we became despondent in the heat. But towards late afternoon, the trail was picked up. The three arch-smugglers, travelling hopelessly on foot, were half-dead with fatigue and exposure. Two revived wonderfully with morphine injections; Dimitrios, who was not an addict, was dehydrated and very ill.

As we were taking our prisoners to their fate, I spoke to an Egyptian police guard sitting beside me, and complimented him upon his stamina; for he had not eaten for nearly twelve hours.

'See this, Effendi, and say nothing more,' he said. Opening a small tin box, he put an opium pill in his mouth. He could not even live without the drug, he told me.

Shortly afterwards, I was in Cairo. Here you would not know Jurgis Sami, the drug-pusher, from any other café-lounger. Nor did I at first. But then he, a long lean man of an oily type, approached me in one of the dimly-lit cafés of Cairo.

The Middle East is full of such men. Today, there is not a single oil-sheikh who has not one, or several, in his entourage. There is no crime that they will not commit; or that they have not, at least, attempted.

Drugs are a favourite game with them. It is estimated

that, between them, they have coaxed into addiction fully one-quarter of the offspring of the millionaire sheikhs.

'Oh, Effendi, dear friend!' he hailed me, 'fancy seeing you in Egypt after so many years! When did you arrive?'

Of course he knew perfectly well that he and I had never met at all. Understanding his motive, I kept quiet and let him share my table. I was on surveillance, hoping to trap bigger fish.

Soon the waiter brought us a pipe. The smell that came from the smoke of the burning hubble-bubble did not please my new acquaintance:

'O, son,' he called to the pipe-bearer. 'This is not the best Turkish hashish!' My host paid well for a new serving of the smouldering drug, as he adjusted the pipe and held the long flexible stem towards me.

It would definitely have been tactically wrong to refuse the proffered pipe; for it was at that café that I was expecting to get information about a load of drugs about to be smuggled into the city.

After taking only two short pulls, trying not to inhale, I returned the pipe to Jurgis. I realised that something potent had travelled up to my brain.

First, there was a slight feeling of intoxication; then it grew rapidly. I was feeling joyous and my eyes seemed to see more clearly. I felt as if I could say something very witty – except that I didn't really want to bother.

Then I did something completely out of character: I landed a slap on Jurgis's bald head, and laughed uproariously at my own joke. Fancy behaving like that towards a total stranger!

And he? His reaction to the drug was more or less the same – we now looked on each other as friends, for were we not hashish smokers? And was he not making a new customer?

I could soon become so conditioned to hashish that I might well, while optimistic under its influence, try something stronger: opium, heroin, perhaps, even cocaine . . .

Seeing the cordiality of our relationship ripening, the waiter quickly brought another pipeful. Jurgis paid for it, and was enjoying it so well that he could no longer sit up on his seat, and rolled to the ground. He was promptly removed to a divan, and thence out of the café and onto the pavement.

Very fortunately, I did not touch hashish any more that night. Egyptian 'hashish' in water-pipes is often a *Majoun*, a mixture of hemp and various other narcotics. The composition varies, and its effects are correspondingly unpredictable.

The next day I was at the café again. So was Jurgis. We now hailed each other as old friends and others greeted us too, for there exists a remarkable freemasonry amongst hashish users. That night I paid for Jurgis's smoke, whilst managing to avoid inhaling it myself. The only other man who seemed to abstain was the café proprietor: I did not like the way he frequently watched me with narrowed eyes.

Determined as I was to play a bolder stroke, I approached him late in the evening and showed him some large-denomination notes in exchange for which I wanted to buy drugs. Price, I said, did not matter. Practically everybody in the café was past caring about what was going on. When fresh smokers came in, their pipes were soon filled, and within half an hour they were lost to their environment.

Descending to an underground passage, the café proprietor took me to a cellar. Passing through it, we came to a sort of kitchen. There, before me, was nothing but a cooking range made of cement, and covered with tiles.

He looked around, and moved something with his foot. Suddenly two men emerged from somewhere, and caught hold of me. They searched me, asking for weapons and papers. They found neither, and as I was a stranger to them, and not even an Egyptian or an Arab, they decided that I could not be an Intelligence man, but was a genuine smuggler or trafficker.

The three stood mute for a moment, while the café-manager slid a slab from the range.

Under it appeared a recess lined with metal. Therein lay some thousands of pounds' worth of the best hashish; only a portion of what was to be sent through the Sinai desert, and on the trail of which even then our men were setting off.

I paid in cash for a quantity and they promised to have the stuff delivered immediately to my flat.

During this conversation, I overheard the destination of the drug-caravan and I made haste to join my unit, on its way to a wadi leading to the shores of the Mediterranean Sea.

By noon the next day, we were hot on the trail of the caravan. Nothing was sighted as we sped past police blockhouses in the desert, but it was difficult going because we only had ordinary cars.

Then, at an outpost, we transferred to desert cars. They were perfect for travel on the soft sand: their wheels did not sink in because the air pressure exerted the same weight per square inch as a camel's foot, and we made better progress.

Towards evening, we spotted a slow-moving camel train, making a dark streak on the pale face of the dunes. They were heading for Damanhur to the south of

Alexandria, where many of the smuggling gangs go; thence contraband can be shipped to Europe fairly easily.

Imagine our disappointment on capturing the caravan, when we found that the camels were not laden at all? Camels were periodically taken for sale like this, to the Egyptian markets.

The only difference was that they were not sheared in the usual manner. The weather that year had not been as hot as usual, the people of the train told us, and the animals needed their fur as protection in the cold desert nights. Fair enough: but where then were those drugs that they were supposed to be smuggling?

By a fortunate accident, someone's hand drifted up to the hump of a camel to pat it. The man was admiring the soft hair of the animal, when his fingers touched something hard. He probed further.

The cameleers were held whilst we searched the animals. On the hump of each camel a patch had been shaved. A slab of dark green stuff was glued to the skin over which the same hair was placed, and carefully combed back.

When it was counted out, that lot of hashish did not cost more than a thousand pounds locally; of which only two or three hundred was to be the share of these Bedouin smugglers. For that they had run their necks into a noose.

On the Alexandria market that quantity could have been sold for nearly £63,000, leaving a net profit of some £59,000 to some fat-bellied international crook, who even now must be sitting smoking his cigar in some European city in peace. His agents do the dirty work.

Before I left the shores of Egypt, I stayed on duty for a spell, and had some minor encounters with smugglers. Once, while sitting in a wayside café, I noticed a Greek kebab vendor who was wearing rather fashionable high-heeled boots.

He refused to remove them when I used my authority to demand that: saying that his socks were full of holes, although I told him that I was not proposing a romantic date.

When we had the footwear ripped open, we found no less than fifty grams of heroin in greaseproof paper packets nestling in the soles and heels.

In another café, we found drugs hidden in such places as the handles of coffee pots, in between hat-racks, in the knobs of brass bedsteads. And, of all places, in the peak of the cap of a sailor we found a pouch with enough cocaine to keep his whole ship supplied for a month.

Another curious case was that of an American tourist, who had swallowed a rubber finger-stall filled with drugs. He could retrieve it in perfect safety. It was attached to one of his teeth by a fine silk thread.

In a colony of addicts, not far from where great liners dropped anchor, I saw the veritable dregs of the world. There were men and boys between the ages of sixteen and thirty – mere shadows, for a single blow would kill them.

They would steal your knife, your spectacles, even your socks if it could get them just one more fix.

Three cases there provided an object lesson: one was a tall, fair-skinned European, the second a Chinese, and the third a West African.

The doctors who visited the colony said that they were in little doubt that there was some genetic factor in addiction. Not that it was exactly racial: but that certain human strains had probably accumulated more addiction-prone genes than others; in much the same way as we find members of national groups to have a similarity in appearance, build and so on.

The drug had not weakened the Chinese man greatly, although he was the oldest addict. But the Ashanti, an addict of only two years' duration, could die from even an ordinary fall down the stairs. The European, so one doctor told me, would not live beyond the age of thirty-five.

Their faces were pale and haggard. They had drooping shoulders, sunken cheeks and chests and their hands trembled as they shook hands with me. The European said that he felt as if his limbs were made of lead.

There were also some Arab labourers there, who had become addicts because their master paid half of their wages in bad food and the other half in drugs. One of the packets of that wage-drug which I examined, consisted almost entirely of white chalk, admixed with a very little dope.

When I left that colony of the living dead, I could not help hating the Dutchman who introduced the drug to Java in the eighteenth century. From there, it had travelled into Formosa, and then into the interior of the East. Working westwards, it found a base in Egypt, from where it now regularly went into Europe.

By the time I was due to leave Egypt, I had had about enough of that adventure. In that frame of mind, even Port Said, that dreadful fleapit, looked quite alluring.

10

Hazards in The Desert

From Port Said I took a boat back to Beirut, for a conference of supposed dervishes from Europe and Asia had been clamouring for guidance, and it was for me to see what I could explain to them of the Sufi Way.

The only thing that happened on the short sea voyage had no relevance to learning or teaching. It was the kind of thing that can often be found in Western newspapers.

It might have been called the Case of the Disappearing Diamond Necklace. It belonged to a French Colonel's wife, and vanished on the first night of our journey.

The necklace was found somehow, though not before an expert pronounced that the jewels were not real diamonds but paste. Was it a case of a fraudulent insurance claim, perhaps? Anyway, the man who had something to do with the affair either jumped into the shallow waters when we neared port – which was considered to be improbable – or managed to gain the shore in a coaling tender, disguised as an Arab longshoreman. And there the matter ended for me.

At Beirut, I hurried to the house of my friend who was a Syrian merchant prince. I found that, after a brief stay which he needed to complete some work in Damascus, I might accompany him into the regions of Dumeir, or perhaps a little way into the range of Jabal-Shargi, to buy camels for the Egyptian market.

He had already paid several hundred gold pieces to the Bedouins as a deposit on these animals; and the time was ripe for the journey to inspect them.

Happy to have the chance of travelling once again through a region which remained more or less unchanged, I was equally pleased to have a few days' rest during which I could study the history and life of Damascus.

Meanwhile, there was work to do. I met a motley crowd of spiritual seekers in one of the great hotels which are such a feature of Beirut. They were drawn from a large number of groups in East and West, which had gathered around some teacher or exponent of what was supposed to be higher spiritual knowledge or development.

In actual fact, though these particular seekers professed their interest in the Sufi philosophy, they had almost no understanding of it. This was clearly because they had equated it with a monkish discipline or a religious group, as known in both conventional and unusual faiths.

Sufi thought and behaviour, I was forced to tell them, could not be vouchsafed to them just because they clamoured for it. Sufis regarded arbitrarily collected mutual-interest groups as very primitive, and unable to cohere in the way necessary for higher learning. They were, I said to the sound of sharp intakes of disapproving breaths, nothing more than forms of diversion, or disguised buying and selling.

There was a hurricane of questions. How did one join the Sufis, then?

One made oneself available, tried to make sure that one did not approach a spurious group – there were a myriad of these – and one served. Service is the keynote of the Sufi Way.

What if one lost interest, or faith, when kept waiting?
Then you were not truly serious.

And, asked another, what if you could not forget your
quest, became obsessed by it – the reverse of falling away?

Then you were not serious either: you were simply
obsessed. Many people are, and it is not Sufism that does it
to them, it is a dozen other things. Obsessionists, like
backsliders, are to be found everywhere . . .

And so it went on, and on, and on. I began to realise that
these people were not spiritual seekers after all. They were
people who had certain psychological needs or desires.
These, in turn, had somehow become attached to the
subject of the dervish group or the Sufi path.

They would have to shed their anxiety and their greed
for knowledge; plus their fear of being left out of
something important.

They needed to be better balanced and to have freed
themselves from the cant and manipulation of false ideas.

Nobody, in East or West, ever seemed to try to tell them
this. They were subjected only to the propaganda and
recruiting ploys of equally ignorant social groups. The
tragedy was that many, if not all, in these groupings
thought themselves to be sincere. They were even thought
to be so by others.

But, until they realised this, these people would never
be able to profit from the real Sufi teaching situation.

For one thing, it was miles away from what they would
imagine to be teaching. They had to unlearn much more
than they were ever likely to be prepared to, before any
learning worth the name could take place.

I fulfilled this part of my mission as well as I could, and
then shook the dust of Beirut from my feet, driving

inland to the glorious city of Damascus, a true pearl of the East.

The next morning I rose early to join the congregation at the Omayyad Mosque, at the eastern end of the Souk Hamidia, 'The Market of Praise'.

The Mosque is undoubtedly one of the most beautiful buildings of its kind and, in magnificence, ranks equal with the Dome of the Rock in Jerusalem. A Roman temple stood on the site, before Theodosius made it into a church – the Church of St. John. In an alcove inside the mosque, I saw a small room where the head of St. John – Yahya, as the Arabs call him – is said to repose to this day.

In its original form this mosque, which is associated with the Caliph Walid, must have had a glorious interior. Moslem authors speak of its floors of the rarest marbles, of prayer niches adorned with precious jewels, and a ceiling inlaid with gold from which hung no fewer than six hundred gold lamps. When I saw it but a short while ago, its interior is moving, even in its present diminished glory.

This Omayyad Mosque, shadowed and intense, felt like the very home of prayer. As the packed masses in front of me rose and fell in the gestures of divine homage, now upstanding, now bowing, now kneeling, the impression was as of trees bending in a gale in a dark forest.

The voice of the prayer leader sounding at intervals, followed by the whispered responses of the worshippers, seemed to be the wind flowing and returning through the wooded aisles of the forest, a susurrant noise more elemental than human.

Above us glittered the lamps in the dome, stars in a sacred firmament, remote eyes gazing down upon this world of supplication.

Could these be the people I had seen in the market, eager, angry, intent on bargaining; these devotees, each profoundly intent on the approach to the divine, each sedulously and reverently occupied, to the exclusion of all else, in atonement for sin, on the acquisition of that holiness which all devout Moslems so deeply desire?

'There is one God.' The solemn words boomed forth in challenging assertion. One God! How faithfully had their coreligionists throughout the generations adhered to the statement of that basic principle!

One God! All of their religion was concentrated in these two solemn words, everything that implies faith, the heart and core of all sanctity.

This is indeed the heart of the Islamic faith, this potent insistence upon the simple and familiar facts of its creed. In its wisdom as a world-wide, unitary community, it admits of no complexities, no theological subtleties.

Its affirmation is simple enough for the least sophisticated, and the wise do not quarrel with its simplicity, because in that very simplicity all else is felt to be contained. The whole of the community and individual loyalty to a Creator is expressed in a few ordinary but telling words.

And the background is as telling as the text. It has an almost Calvinistic bareness. Only here and there does the innate expressiveness of the Orient display itself in a prayer-rug of rich and living colour, a splash of radiance against the spotless pavement, or a suspicion of faded gold on wall or pillar.

Yet there is little of monastic bleakness. The spirit which informs the place is much too bounteous in its overflowing warmth to make for a coldness of the atmosphere. The reflection of that fervour seems to be caught by the snowy walls; its heat and fragrance ascend to the white dome.

And here all men are equal, the millionaire and the beggar, the professor, the hawker, the farmer and the simple tradesman, all are returned to the status of brothers: all alike creatures of Allah.

In the East, I realised with a powerful intensity, people do not dress up to go to church. They go, and they go daily, in the clothes of their condition, profession or trade. They enter the mosque out of the wayfaring of the street, not as nobles or merchants or soldiers, but as humans seeking atonement and communion with their Maker. No pews are reserved for their private use...

Soon after the congregational prayer, I looked closely at the mosque; and noted that it is very unlike many others. It is rectangular rather than square or circular: perhaps four hundred feet by one hundred and thirty; more or less like a basilica with two rows of columns.

The niches beneath the roof are of stained glass. The beauty of its design is fully maintained by its courtyard. A double-storied arcade runs around it; and around the Dome of the Treasury, where the funds of the mosque are said once to have been kept.

It was just after eight in the morning, and the din of the bazaars – shops there open at eight and shut at sundown – was like the distant humming of bees. But before I went to walk the bazaars, I paid my respects to the tomb of Salahuddin Ayyubi – the great Sultan Saladin, Richard the Lionheart's opponent in the Crusades. It is in a narrow lane, its outer aspect appearing neglected, but the inside was clean and peaceful.

And thence to the many bazaars for which Damascus is justly famous throughout the East.

There are, for instance, the spice bazaars. Enter and you might think to have arrived in a garden of flowers rather than somewhere in the heart of a great city. Scents, herbs and dry blossoms are for sale at every booth and shop.

Further on is the blacksmiths' bazaar, and then the Long Bazaar, the longest street in the whole city; nearby is the bazaar of the goldsmiths and the silk bazaar; every nook and corner of each overflowing with humanity. Brisk buying and selling is going on everywhere; not for nothing is Damascus called the Mart of the Orient.

And why not? In the West the shop is only a shop, even if it be a department store. There is about as much mystery adhering to it as to a railway station. People go there to buy things and that is all, unless it be a village store, where people can exchange local gossip.

But in the East, the bazaar, though chiefly and ostensibly for the purchase of goods, is an institution – a political club, an exchange, a resort of the folk, and last, a cavern of secrets as profound as those of Delphi itself.

Anything may happen to you in a bazaar. I do not mean anything alarming or dangerous, for the tales of terror and wonder circulated throughout the West about these places are absurdly exaggerated. Whoever you are, you may walk through most bazaars as safely as in Burlington Arcade, and perhaps with more assurance that your pocket will not be rifled.

All the same, the bazaar is the gate of adventure and you may see or overhear things there of which even the boldest romancer would not dream.

Those parts of any big Eastern bazaar dedicated to the sale of fresh goods and provisions differ very little from their counterparts in London or Paris. It is when you come to the sections where garments, metalwork, furnishings, jewels and ornaments change hands that you reach the real bazaar of tradition.

Here you can observe those famous scenes of chaffering

and bargaining which, like fiction serials, are 'continued', sometimes over weeks and months.

Here are to be heard the rhetorical appeals to Allah as to the unspotted honesty of the vendors, as well as the sarcastic replies of the turbaned customers.

Those two men whom you see yonder, apparently arguing over the price of a rug from Tabriz, are in reality discussing the affairs of a visiting merchant of whose financial status they are not convinced.

The little man talking to the big fellow in the fez is not trying to sell him the small copper tray he handles so nervously, but is actually questioning him about the amount of baksheesh the police will require from him in some affair or other which has recently come to prominence.

That pearl which the jeweller, in black jacket and turban, is holding in his palm beneath the hooked nose of the man in uniform may get sold by Ramadan, or more possibly it may not; if in his anxiety his eloquence runs dry.

And, wherever you turn, there is an echo of whispers, for the bazaar is the greatest whispering-gallery in the world. What it is all about you will never entirely guess: indeed the bazaar itself cannot tell.

It is the echo of the inherent mystery of the East, the shadow of sound, the spectre of opinion and hearsay, perhaps full-charged with momentous truth and probability, maybe signifying nothing.

In a way, the bazaar is a hive where the bees have stopped working, but where the hum of an apparent business goes on incessantly.

One half of it is in the world of everyday, the other half in a region where dreams and fancies find us when we leave the beaten tracks of life.

And was it a coincidence, or a yearning, I wondered,

that country folk in the West, whenever they can, choose to hold 'a bazaar'?

My friend the merchant Sheikh, although a keen business man, still gloried in the traditional pageantry of his forbears.

Syrians are intensely, and justly, proud of their past history; and despite the fact that we must soon be taking the desert route into the heart of north-eastern Syria, the Sheikh persuaded me to wait a few days longer.

At the close of Ramadan – the month of fasting – the Bairam Feast, the Festival of the Fast Breaking, is celebrated. Then, many Emirs of the desert and others from less barren lands, would come to Damascus in all their Royal state – so to speak: and the procession of even one of them was certainly worth seeing.

These Emirs have retained their semi-independence. Even the French Mandate after the First World War, and then the present Republic, have had no effect upon the hoary tradition of courtesy and precedence accorded to these chieftains.

Many of them were fabulously wealthy, and even retained a small army of their tribal followers; the procession of one such I was destined to see on the morning of the Festival.

I stood outside the Souk Hamidia, when practically all important Sheikhs with their retainers had left the mosque after the customary service. Amidst tense excitement we waited for the last and the most superb procession to pass.

It started with the trumpet fanfare – not trumpets such as you may hear outside Buckingham Palace, but brass holding a significance a world away in their unusual clamour.

Small atabals, then their cousins the giant drums, beat out a rhythm that sent the heart pounding. Then came the light clattering of twice a hundred hoofs, and the procession passed down the winding street into the square.

Here was a magnificence not to be seen elsewhere – not the rude blaze of barbarism nor the staid and sombre brilliance of European pageantry. Here was the grandeur which came from a civilization going back twelve centuries or more; and, before that, who knows to what ancient Eastern empire: snow-white horses, turbans and flashing steel, warrior faces and bolt upright, soldierly shapes.

The music crashed out in a fantastic march. The great drums pulsated like thunder, crushed into rhythm by some unbelievable force – such music as the Crusaders might have heard when they clashed with the horsemen of the Sultan, music that would turn a churl into a paladin in mind by the magic of its blood-churning appeal.

The dark faces smiled exultantly, the white teeth flashed. What a beautiful people this was, heroic, not cramped into the attitudes and postures of business or the humped shapes of labour, but triumphantly human and alive, a nation of fighters and chieftains!

Like grey-brown ships billowing upon a foam of white horses, wallowed the camels, each carrying its cargo of nobility, housed in gold and silver and silk – wise-looking animals, impassive, their heads turned upwards at the angle of hauteur.

Yet they were not more impassive than the chiefs they carried, each sitting cross-legged in his litter, smothered in medieval finery, unseeing, perhaps unhearing.

Sons of a hundred generations of power: their forefathers may have looked back on yet another hundred

184

generations at the time that the Conquest brought its half-tamed Vikings to rule in England.

Before each of the turreted beasts tripped a bevy of sword-dancers, displaying those strange movements which their kind brought from ancient Egypt, possibly three thousand years ago.

The warlike eyes shone; the jingle of silver decorations was surely even older than that temple on the hill yonder; these eyes more fathomless than the dark river which flowed beneath it.

At each fresh outburst of the wild and fevered music they made new and even more extraordinary movements: dancing not with their feet alone as Europeans tend to do, but with their bodies, their eyes, their very hair, as they rent the empty air with their naked blades.

The crowds shouted their acclamation, no less ardently because the nobles took no notice of them. In the East, only lesser people take notice of crowds or acclamation: that is the abiding aristocratic tradition.

Modern politicans, dictators and the like, orchestrate and demand loud homage. Obligingly, the masses give it. Their true reverence however, is reserved for the quieter nobles, who accept their tributes but show no sign of excitement themselves.

Then came the desert warriors, hardy-looking fellows, lithe and limber, who would give a good account of themselves anywhere: soldiers who were the sons of soldiers, not conscripts. Rather they were men whose ranks had known the fighter's trade for generations; long before Europe was split into nation-states and who preferred close-quarters fighting with steel to modern 'stone-throwing by gunpowder'.

Little by little, the music was swallowed up in the distance. The great drums still rumbled like a far-off cannonade: the trumpets turned to fairy clarions; only the undulating camels' backs still visible through their haze of dust.

The pageant took on the appearance of dream – a dream that will long remain in my memory as the recollection of a people's magnificence.

At last we were on the move, going north-east. The rocky defiles, mixed with loose sand and crags, lay still under a baking sun.

Eight camels laden with food, water and three tents followed the Arab mounts of the Sheikh and myself: a third horse on which the Sheikh had laden silver coins, the price of the camels which we were going out to buy, was led by my host's slave, Bin Kafur.

Our train dipped and rose between the sand-dunes and the waterless ravines; and in that great emptiness I realized once more how little time means in the desert. Life loses its customary meaning in this wilderness.

There man is made to know how infinitely small, how utterly small, he is in the vastness of a desert – a nearly waterless stretch where life depends on water and on the stamina of man and beast to do without it!

Nothing lives there, almost nothing grows. Only here and there do you see the *rimth* bush with its needle-shaped leaves between which tiny white flowers are trying to show their faces – as if begging for a drop of dew.

The *rimth* is well-named, meaning, in Arabic, raft; and in its precarious hold upon the desert sand, this charming shrub does indeed seem something like a raft at sea.

Finally, we pitched our tents, and as the territory of wandering Bedouins was now not far off, watchmen were posted to keep guard throughout the night.

Next morning, the dark desert awoke to the sun's touch and soon the air seemed to glitter like a blade of steel. After a hurried breakfast and the morning prayer, we rode some nine miles due east before descending a stark and boulder-strewn gully, to reach a desert town where there was a *caravanserai* – a rest-house. There the balance of the Sheikh's money was to be given to those who had been buying camels for him.

It was as well that we attained the heights overlooking the townlet before dark. There they told us that but a few hours ago, another tribe had attacked them. Word had got around that we had already arrived, with bags of silver coins.

The Western mind may conjure up wonderful and visionary details of the *caravanserai* or *khan*. To the clerk from Battersea or the grocer in Omaha, the very name is associated with a wild rapture of coloured magnificence which outshines the scenes in films of the *Arabian Nights*. But beautiful names have their own drawbacks, and a woman may be called Gwendolyn or Cleopatra and yet fail to fulfil the appellation's promise.

There is a famous story of two lovers in the East: their names are Layla and Majnun. Apparently the lady's appearance was not all that her besotted lover thought her: hence, almost as famous, there is the proverb: 'You have to look at Layla only with the eyes of Majnun.'

And this, I am afraid, is the case with the caravanserai. Hollywood, Victorian novelists and its musical name have been the making of it. But indeed that name signifies nothing more than a 'house or lodging for travellers by caravan'. One might as well expect visionary delights in the waiting-room of a small railway-station.

This benighted town's caravanserai, like many others where I had stayed, was composed of one-story adobe buildings, arranged around a courtyard where the camels and asses were stalled. The buildings were divided into places for sleeping and public apartments for eating and converse.

No doubt many inns and hostelries in medieval Europe were of this pattern: those hospices and auberges where pilgrims enjoyed rest and refreshment on the stages of their journey. I am loath to shatter dreams, but frankly, few of these places were particularly sanitary or free from attentive insect life.

These things notwithstanding, this rest-house was not without a strange if distorted quality of its own. Its ugliness was indeed a certain kind of beauty; if not fair, it was at least fantastic in the manner of a Flemish interior.

The grouping of weird personalities, their grotesque gestures, the vivid dark faces, the strangeness of unusual postures, the splash of unfamiliar colours; combined to make a canvas of the oddest life against the sombre background of softly shadowed walls.

No painter in his senses, I thought, but would rush for his palette and brushes, if he were permitted, in such surroundings. I thought, sadly, that none such had ever seen a scene quite like this, and none was ever to glimpse this part of the very essence of the East.

Here, where every corner had its praying suppliant, where every other square yard of floor was occupied by small circles discussing politics or religion, or gravely consuming the slender bread and onion diet of the Eastern traveller; past and present are commingled like light and darkness.

I do not think the world will ever behold an Orient where the caravanserai is not. For we cannot criss-cross the desert for ever with railroads or motorways: sand is mightier than any engineering.

It is not improbable that for a time the aircraft, the car and the motor-bus may displace the camel. Even so, the caravanserai will remain. It allows a freedom of intercourse which even the best hotels do not possess and with which they cannot compete. Indeed, people who use hotels frequently generally hate them: the very opposite of the reaction to the serai, tiny inhabitants notwithstanding.

It is this freedom of intercourse which the sons of Asia love; this opportunity for debate and the interchange of idea and experience which has made the caravanserai as dear to them as his club, inn or restaurant is to the European.

When the Sheikh had finished his business with the Bedouins, we all shared in his hospitality with the customary celebration of sweetmeats all round, and the story-teller was relating a long-winded tale. Suddenly there was much hammering at the gate of the caravanserai.

Men ran hither and thither in confusion seeking their weapons: everybody was still jittery because of the recent desert raid. But the mystery was soon solved when the watchman shouted from his tower to say that it was only the 'reformed brigand' who sought admittance.

Ali, the one-eyed ex-brigand, was demanding the blood of Selim. The one-eyed Ali had argued with Selim the muleteer until what there was of his professional patience had run out. The quarrel, being about a woman, was of the type which could only be ended by the shedding of blood.

My friend the Sheikh, however, would have none shed in his presence: this was against etiquette – so a duel was agreed upon. Ali insisted that it was to take place there and then, in the centre of the serai. So the Sheikh withdrew, affecting not to have heard this preposterous demand, to attend, as he said, to private devotions.

The two bared their scimitars, and immediately joined issue before I realized what was happening.

The scimitar is a deadly weapon and a sweeping blow with it is usually decisive if it connects. Arab fencing involves the whole body and a cut at the legs is usually met by leaping higher than the opponent's blade.

As the combatants met, their blades flashed and whistled in the silver light of each shadowy pass; clashed, disengaged and swooped earthward for a fatal leg-blow, the duellists leaping upward at each pass like a pair of fighting-cocks.

If Selim was the more agile, he certainly had fewer tricks of desert fencing at his command than his wary enemy, whose single gleaming eye again and again probed the weakest points in his foe's defence.

While the fighting continued, a running commentary of raillery and sneers issued from the duellists, who hurled at each other every objurgation and evil epithet in their very extensive repertoires. Once Ali leapt none too high and Selim's blade shore clean through a couple of his toes.

I would have thought the wound was bad enough to halt even the most courageous, but though it bled profusely, the single-eyed swordsman carried on as if nothing had happened and, indeed, redoubled his efforts.

That a man of well over sixty should be able to stand up to such a gruelling test says much for the hardihood and valour of the men of the desert; and as, with greater ardour than before, Ali pressed his adversary ever more closely, an expression of increasing strain began to appear in Selim's swarthy features and he steadily gave ground.

Now the elder swordsman saw an opportunity and struck savagely at his enemy's eyes. Selim successfully blocked the stroke, which, therefore, was never fully delivered. At the decisive moment when the stroke should have connected, Ali's blade swerved downward, swift as the descent of lightning.

A moment later, Selim, badly wounded, lay gasping on the grass.

The 'brigand' had won his bride. I saw him call to a woman whose presence I had not noticed in the cara-vanserai, and, claiming her as his wife, he took her out into the darkness of the night.

The actual business of buying the camels had been completed, the money paid and eighteen animals had already been delivered to us. The Sheikh, thinking it unsafe to tarry any longer in that place, decided to push on to yet another northern village and to leave the Bedouins to deliver the rest of the camels to him in a fortnight.

Another day's march of some ten dreary miles, in and out of rocky heights, brought us to an encampment where there was another transaction to be negotiated.

But a most extraordinary sight met our eyes before we had an opportunity to talk business with Sheikh Israr. A massive confrontation was developing.

As we approached the valley, we saw that it was black with people; such a concourse as I would not have believed that that sparsely populated region could have supported.

On the slopes surrounding the centre of the vale the men of several tribes were gathered, each group with its own insignia, and marshalled under its emirs, the battle-leaders.

The clamour of speech was everywhere, rising in little tides and waves, from which at times a spray of shriller shouts and cries leapt up. The sight was like a flower-garden of parterres: the greens, blues and scarlets of garments and banners blossoming against the dark hillsides in their own sombre hues.

Then came a group of Sheikhs, robed in brown, bearded and solemn. Taking their stand upon a small hillock, they consulted for a space. Then one of them stepped forward from the rest and raised an arm high.

Instantly a great hush fell upon the assembled clans. The elder's voice rose and fell in a monotonous sing-song at first, almost like that of the voice from a minaret calling the prayer. Then it broke suddenly into a loud note of denunciation.

We listened as the words from his bellowing throat came clearly to us in the still air. He thundered at those who had broken faith with his people. He lashed them with a whip of words which acted upon the men like brands of fire, fanning the dryness of their resentment into a blaze of wrath. There was a clatter of arms, of muskets and lances, like the passage of a gale through a forest.

Realizing the dangerous effect of his oratory, the speaker faltered. He had, it seemed to me, almost over-stepped the limits necessary to his purpose. It was probably not his intention to goad the people to a fury which he might not later be able to control. After all, chiefdom is defined hereabouts as 'the power to bind and to loose.' Chiefs needed both capacities.

He raised a restraining hand. He spoke more temperately now. But, instead of calming the tribespeople, these words appeared to have an even more infuriating effect.

Perhaps a half-excuse for an enemy is the most effective way of rousing an audience to a full frenzy of hatred and enmity and – perhaps the elder knew it. Again he altered his tone.

We drew nearer, to listen as he harangued his own

group: 'So,' he cried, 'if your murmurs express your true feelings, if you have been concealing your natural sentiments, why do you stand there inactive and hesitating? You have your remedy and it is not that of the spectator!

'You are aware how you have been insulted, jeered at, called by opprobrious names, laughed at as women and cowards. And you only whisper like the little breeze that hails the sunrise!

'How gentle you are, how long-suffering! What wonder is it that your enemies see in you those feminine graces which they admire so much in their wives, their sisters and their daughters? In your patience you are beautiful. Alas, though, that beauty should be so feeble, so unmanly!'

The old fellow had gone all out, after all. From the first it was obvious that trouble was likely: and the roars of rage which greeted his latest sally easily confirmed earlier fears.

During his speech the massed bodies of his men on the hillside had begun to move in an agitated manner. Now they were swaying to and fro. Warriors from the rear ranks were running from side to side like creatures possessed. Lances and rifles were flourished, warlike slogans were being shouted from raucous throats.

The speaker ceased. His work was done, and done well. The tribes broke order and surged towards the hillock, their faces distorted with fury, their eyes rolling savagely. Great indeed is the power of oratory, especially when its ideas coincide with, or manifest, popular opinion and intention.

Having watched all this, my host spoke in a husky voice. 'Brother! If we are wise we shall make no camp near them; but will return to Damascus forthwith.'

'And water, O Sheikh?' I asked. We had only a meagre supply left.

'Allah provides for the sons of the desert,' he said, and

under the darkness of a sinking moon we turned our camel train westward.

That there was considerable unease throughout the eastern desert and up to the regions of Jabal – at Shargi every man's hand was raised against his fellow – was all too clear to us.

We, being mere town Arabs – so to speak – wished to take no part in inter-tribal quarrels; so water or no water, we pushed on westward with all possible speed. Two camels had to be slaughtered on the way, to use the store of liquid which these animals carried.

'If we get through the passes of the outer range, brother,' muttered the Sheikh to me on the second day, his voice cracked with thirst, 'we shall be safe!' But that was not to be.

We were now negotiating the dreaded Tawil Pass and there were many marauders here who did not care whom they looted.

The wildness and loneliness of that pass is hard to conceive. Immense and jagged rocks, which seemed to have been distorted into shapes peculiarly monstrous by the more evil tendencies in the forces of nature, overshadowed our way; seeming to make the night still darker and more terrible. I shall call it evil, if that does not label me as over-imaginative . . .

We had hoped to negotiate this defile before nightfall, but the slow, dragging progress of the caravan's tail where the older camels lagged behind, had slowed our progress severely.

The long, snakelike body of the camel-train had scarcely been swallowed up in the gloom of the pass when suddenly a noise like the crack of a giant whip resounded through the darkness.

I knew that sound only too well. It was the explosion of home-made gunpowder in a muzzle-loading musket.

For a moment the whole length of the caravan, stopped and stood stock-still, frozen into immobility.

Then the Gehennam of Shaitan, the Black One, itself appeared to be let loose. From the rocks above, screaming fiendishly, ragged dusty shapes poured down upon us, firing as they came. That most of their bullets sang over our heads didn't matter, for they caused nearly as much confusion as though each one had found its billet.

Many of us were armed and were soon blazing away into the darkness, but they could have effected little or no damage. I unshipped my Browning and set it going too, to show willing, rather than in the hope of warding off the attack.

For some moments these exchanges took place. Then they were among us, furious men, flourishing long-barrelled matchlocks, clubbing us with their butts, jabbing with razor-sharp lances.

A caravan is as easily frightened as a flock of pigeons and the weird yells and war-cries uttered by the attackers were echoed by the shrieks of our demoralised cameleers who now ran off, helter-skelter through the darkness.

The camels, horses and asses, also terrified by the hub-bub, broke for freedom; but, pressed into a mass by the confines of the narrow defile, could not get far, and remained plunging, kicking, neighing, braying and roaring, each according to its kind, in the wide hollow.

After about five minutes of this inferno, it became clear that only some twenty men had attacked us – and they were badly armed.

Those of us who possessed rifles or revolvers, and who were not of the cameleer type, gathered together behind boulders, in approved defensive posture, and began to pour effective fire into the thin ranks of the attackers.

Little by little the bandits gave way. Their ancient guns, mostly muzzle-loaders, did not allow them to fire with anything like the speed of our modern weapons. Yet, with all that noise and fighting at close-quarters, it seemed a miracle that there were no fatalities, although six of our men and two of the attackers were wounded. Three of the enemy were captured.

It was while I was searching for my camel that the sequel happened. I had left the three bandits alive, but when I returned there was no sign of them.

When I asked the Sheikh what had become of them, he pointed wordlessly to an ugly chasm in the rocks. I peered into its black profundity, but could see nothing but the velvet surface of darkness. The rent in the rock seemed indeed 'deeper than plummet ever sounded'. This was life, and death, in that wild land. I remounted and we were off once more.

The attackers had gambled and lost. It might have been *rouge* for us, but it was very much *noir* for them.

APPENDIX

The Eleven Points of Recognition

In answer to questions from Western students, these are the indications of a genuine Sufi Master, according to the Grand Dervish Council.

The Sufi Master:

1 Has a strong sense of humour, and shows it frequently

2 Wears, most of the time, the clothes of the country wherein he lives

3 Speaks that country's language perfectly, has no foreign accent

4 Supports himself by his own labour

5 Knows at least one of the classical languages (Persian and Arabic)

6 Ordinarily eats the wholesome food of the country where he dwells

7 Does not indulge in, or require, chants, repetitions, prayers, etc. as supposed parts of Sufi behaviour

8 Shuns music within the Sufi context

9 Has no physical relations or familiarity with his disciples

10 Does not allow his disciples to leave the world or cut communication with their relatives and friends

11 Recognises that all Sufi 'orders' and 'books' are temporary formulae, and not to be applied automatically at all times and to all people.